Translated from the French by:
Adam Stephenson, Susan Ashcroft, Victoria Erbin,
Patricia Kessler, Thomas Kessler.

COPTIC
FABRICS

Marie-Hélène Rutschowscaya

ADAM
BIRO

Note to the readers :
For a better visibility,
certain subjects have been
enlarged slightly.

© 1990, Editions Adam Biro
17, rue du Louvre,
75001 Paris
France

TABLE
OF CONTENTS

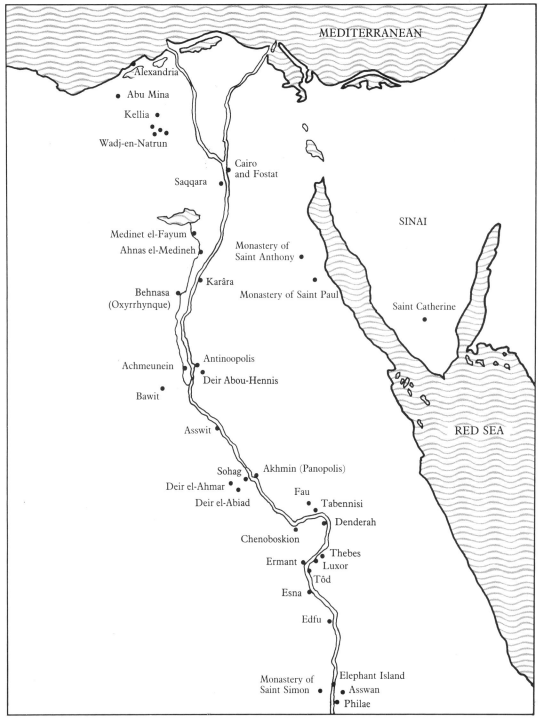

MEDITERRANEAN

Alexandria

Abu Mina

Kellia

Wadj-en-Natrun

Cairo
and Fostat

Saqqara

SINAI

Medinet el-Fayum

Ahnas el-Medineh

Monastery of
Saint Anthony

Karâra

Behnasa
(Oxyrrhynque)

Monastery of Saint Paul

Saint Catherine

Antinoopolis

Achmeunein

Deir Abou-Hennis

Bawit

RED SEA

Asswit

Akhmin (Panopolis)

Sohag

Deir el-Ahmar

Fau

Deir el-Abiad

Tabennisi

Denderah

Chenoboskion

Thebes

Ermant

Luxor

Tôd

Esna

Edfu

Monastery of
Saint Simon

Elephant Island

Asswan

Philae

N. PERCHE

Map of Coptic Egypt

INTRODUCTION

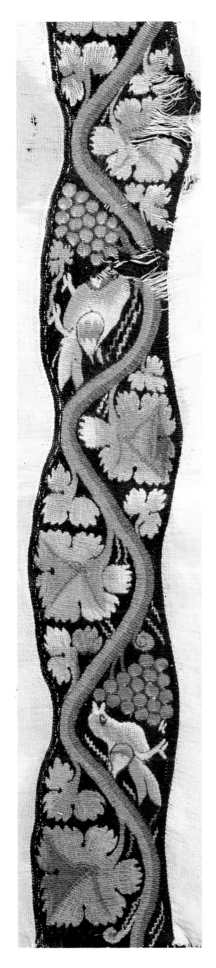

For the general public, Coptic Egypt is the world of Coptic weavers, whose work was so spectacularly brought to light by archeologists at the turn of the century. The 1900 Paris World Fair[1] revealed to art lovers a previously unsuspected genre, surprising not only for the size of the discoveries but also for their quality and technical originality.

Since then, museums and temporary exhibitions have displayed thousands of Coptic fabrics; collections of Coptic objects are regularly put on the market at auctions which bring them to the attention of an ever wider public; and art and archeology books about the period never fail to make room for Coptic Egypt and weaving techniques.

The growing artistic appeal of Coptic textiles is mainly due to their "primitive" look. Their popular, naive style is as unclassical as could be and has the charm of craft objects, whose attraction does not fluctuate with changes in fashion.

Just as the cubists were drawn to African art, other modern artists seem to have been attracted by the pictorial style of Coptic fabrics.[2] The sculptor, August Rodin had a collection of them which is now preserved at the Rodin Museum in Paris.[3] Great modern collectors have naturally aquired specimens for their "modernity" and affinities with contemporary work.[4]

Galloons decorated with birds and foliage
Tapestry and tabby. Linen and wool
4th century
71.5 x 33.5 cm
London, Victoria and Albert Museum; inv. 819-1905
Interwoven yarns of varying color gradations create a modeling effect.

HISTORICAL OUTLINE

 Sandwiched between the two great periods of Egyptian history, the Age of the Pharaohs and that of Islam, Coptic Egypt is not named, like them, for its king and its religion but, more prosaically, after a geographical point, the country's center of worship.

The words "Copt" and "Coptic" are derived from the Greek "Aigyptios," itself formed from the name of the ancient sanctuary of Memphis, "Het-ka-Ptah," (the House of Ka Ptah), the dynastic god of Egypt from the time of the Old Kingdom. The Greeks gave this name to the inhabitants of the land of the Pharaohs.

After the Arab conquest in the middle of the 7th century, the word was reduced to its consonants. In Arabic script, which does not have vowels, the word became *qbt* which, in our prounounciation, becomes Copt.

When the Arabs arrived in Egypt in 641/642, the country was entirely Christianized. The word "Copt" referred therefore not only to the inhabitants, but also to the Christians, in opposition to the Muslim invaders. In the natural course of things, the term ended up by being applied to the religious rite followed in Egypt and, by extension, to the same rite as borrowed by the Nubians, Ethiopians and Armenians. According to tradition, Saint Mark began the evangelization of Egypt in the first half of the first century A.D. The process continued gradually and was practically completed by the middle of the 5th century. Between these dates the country went from the domination of Rome (30 B.C.) to that of Byzantium (395 A.D.). This foreign yoke, and particularly that of the Byzantine Greeks, was always resented by the Egyptians, who tried to revolt several times. The opposition to Byzantine political power was one of the major causes of their separation in the religious domain. In 451, the Council of Chalcedon condemned Monophysitism, the doctrine of Eutyches, a monk of Constantinople, according to which Christ's humanity was only apparent, not real. The Patriarch of Alexandria, Dioscorus, eventually supported this doctrine. An interminable rivalry began between the Orthodox Copts, who followed Disocorus, and the Melchite Copts (from the Syriac word for king), partisans of the Byzantine emperor.

The history of the Copts does not end abruptly in the middle of the 7th century. In spite of some difficult periods, like the persecutions of the Caliph Al Hakim (1006-1020), the Copts have always been regarded as the intellectual elite of the Egyptian nation, and occupied many of the highest functions in the administration.

Nevertheless, the heavy taxes which burdened non-Muslims led many of the Copts to embrace the religion of the victors. By the middle of the 9th century, they had lost their numerical superiority; today, the Copts make up only about 10 % of the population.

The word "Coptic" not only designates an ethnic group and a church; it is also the name of a language, with all its unifying and civilizing power. The first traces of Coptic writing appeared in the 2nd century B.C., and it flourished from the 3rd century A.D. It is composed of the Greek alphabet with seven additional signs borrowed from the last phase of ancient Egyptian writing, called "demotic." These stand for sounds which Greek letters can not indicate. It was the simplification brought about by the adoption of the Greek alphabet that enabled Jean-François Champollion, by assuming a continuity of syntax and vocabulary with the ancient Egyptian language, to decipher the hieroglyphics. From the beginning of the 8th century, Arabic was proclaimed the official language and Coptic was strictly confined to the liturgical function it still retains, in part, today.

There is, however, another sense to the word "Coptic." During the 4th century, a new artistic style began to make itself felt, particularly in sculpture. The earliest examples of this have been brought to light in Middle Egypt, at Ahnas el Medineh and Oxyrhynchus. At that time, the country was still largely pagan. The word "Coptic" is therefore used to refer to the Egyptians, both pagan and Christian, as well as to their artistic production from the 4th century to the end of the 12th, when the arts and crafts of the Egyptian Christians, now often copying Byzantine and Islamic models, finally faded out.

Before this date, however, Christian affairs flourished under the Muslim governors. The Copts played a dominant role in the development of an Islamic art in Egypt. Thanks to the renown of their art and the skill of their craftsmen, they were even called to the great building projects of the time in Medina and Damascus. "Coptic tradition interracted with Muslim dynamism and the two fused. It was the Copts, however, who, by the longevity of their workshops and wealth of their traditions, had the greater influence on Muslim art in Egypt."[5]

In the light of this information, we can distinguish three periods in the history and art of the Copts:

- 4th century - mid-5th century A.D. : development of Coptic art,largely pagan;

- mid-5th century - 8th century : flourishing of

Square with quail
Tapestry and weft-looped weave
Linen and wool
4-5th centuries
72 x 66 cm
Haifa, Haifa Museum; inv. 6041
This square is inserted in a fragment of weft woven linen
which probably belonged to a larger piece (perhaps a blanket)
decorated with several squares.
The quail motif appears frequently
in Coptic fabrics, mosaics and paintings.

Coptic art as it gradually becomes Christian;

   - 8th century - end of the 12th : Coptic art under
   Arab domination.

Beneath the commotion of political events, old Egypt did not change so very much. The Nile flowed on, majestic as ever, through the same deserts, past the same monuments of ancient Kings, occupied now by Greeks, now Romans, now Christians. The monastic foundations of the latter often adapted themselves to the ancient stuctures, which had many analogies with Coptic churches (e.g.,the great festal hall of Thutmosis III at Karnak, the sanctuary of the temple at Luxor, the court of the temple of Ramses III at Medinet Habu). The first anchorites*, St. Macarius, St. Anthony, St. Paul of Thebes, etc. - took possession of caves and ancient tombs often far away from the Nile valley. Monastic foundation formed around them and their fame drew thousands of monks and ascetics into the desert, where they lived in complete solitude (the anchorites) or communally (the coenobites*).

Alexandria (founded by Alexander the Great in 330 B.C.), which had been the administrative capital of Egypt under the Greeks, naturally became the seat of the Patriarchate. The inhabitants of the rest of the country were mostly fellahin (peasants), but in the big cities of the nomes (regions) like Akhmin, Antinoopolis, Assiut or Herakleopolis, two populations lived side by side, often ignoring one another,the orthodox Copts remaining profoundly attached to their national identity. As Jean Maspero says, describing the Coptic reaction to the Council of Chalcedon, "The condemnation of their pope was not only an ecclesiastical event and an attack on their pride as a Christian elite, it was an outrage to the whole nation; for the Patriach had rapidly become a kind of representative of the indigenous race against the central authority."[6]

1. *Les costume en Egypte,* 1900.
2. *Coptic Art,* 1955
3. *Sublime indigo,* 1987, N° 109-110,112, 114-115.
4. *La rime et la raison,* 1984, p. 238-239, p. 323-324, n° 105-107.
5. Edward PAUTY, 1930, p. VII
6. Jean MASPERO, 1923, p. 37.

* The words followed by an asterisk appear in the glossary on page 152.

IMPORTANT DATES

2nd century BC	Appearance of Coptic writing
30 B.C.	Octavian conquers Egypt, which becomes a Roman province, directly dependent on him.
40-49 A.D.	According to tradition, St. Mark evangelizes Egypt
approx. 180 A.D.	Founding of Didascaleum at Alexandria
247-264	Dionysus Bishop of Alexandria
251-356	Life of St. Anthony
284-305	The great persecution of Diocletian marks the beginning of the "Age of Matyrs" corresponding to the beginning of the Coptic calendar.
313	Edict of Milan : recognition of Christianity
346	Life of St. Pachomius, founder of the first convent, at Tabennisi, in upper Egypt
328-373	Athanasius Bishop of Alexandria
350	Translation of the bible into Coptic.
380	Christianity proclaimed the state religion by Theodosius I.
381	Creation of Diocese* of Egypt.
391	Prohibition of pagan religions by Theodosius.
385-412	Destruction of the serapeum* of Alexandria under the patriarchate of Theophilus.
395	Death of Theodoius I. The Empire is divided between his two sons. Arcadius (395-408) received the Eastern Empire, whose capital is Byzantium.
412-444	St. Cyril Patriarch of Alexandria.
431	Council of Ephesus.
444-451	Dioscorus Patriarch of Alexandria
451	The Council of Chalcedon condemns monophysitism, the doctrine which affirms that Christ has only one, divine, nature. It was consequently held to deny the reality of His incarnation and passion. The Christians of Egypt maintain the doctrine and break away from the official church.
538	Deposition of Therodorus, Patriarch of Alexandria.
543	The temple of Philae closed to the nobades*, whose pagan religion had previously been tolerated within its walls.
619-629	Occupation of Egypt by the Persians.
631	Cyrus Patriarch of Alexandria.
641	Conquest of Egypt by the Arabs. The general Amr ibn el As enters Babylon and founds Fostat (642).
658-750	Umayyad dynasty in Damascus. Egypt is ruled by governors.
750-868	Abbasid dynasty in Baghdad and Samara.
868-905	Tulunid period. Independence of the governors.
969-1171	Fatimid dynasty in Cairo.
1047-1077	The Coptic Patriarch, Christodulos transfers the seat of the Patriarchate from Alexandria to Cairo.
1171-1250	Ayyubid dynasty.

COPTIC
FABRICS
TODAY

FROM BURIAL CLOTHES...

 Nearly all the Coptic fabrics known today were found in tombs, where the dead lay dressed in their finest clothes. The exceptional good state of preservation of materials which elsewhere are perishable (textiles, wood, leather and other organic substances) is due to the dry Egyptian climate and the sandy soil, in which the tombs were dug always a long way from damp, cultivated fields. For this reason, Egyptian fabrics offer us very full and precious information about weaving techniques in Antiquity.

The ancient ritual of mummification, which for several thousand years had been considered indispensable for the survival of body and soul, was gradually abandoned during the 3rd century A.D. Instead, people were buried according to their rank and function, the humblest in simple graves, more important figures in masonry tombs. The bodies were rarely put in coffins, but rested on wooden planks or directly on the earth. They were wrapped in shrouds held in place by narrow bandages, thus imitating the previous mummies.

There were sometimes several of these shrouds, completely white or with woven decoration, each covering a different part of the body. In a tomb in the monastery of St. Epiphanius at Thebes, however, the cloth was broad enough to be rolled up and folded into a cushion over the feet and the face; it was laced up with sewn tapes.[1]

Often, pieces of wall hangings or shawls were obviously used, for the ribbons have left a lattice of marks all over the surface of the cloth. "The dead person was buried in clothes whose number and splendor were in proportion to his fortune; some had as many as four tunics. In the same way, the body covering was more or less meticulously cared for. But however opulent the garments, the procedure was the same for all: after being dressed in even the most richly embroidered clothes, the body was wrapped in one or two shrouds of white cloth. A layer of palm fibers, and finally, to hold it all together, one last shroud. Particular attention was paid to the head, which was given a very characteristic rectangular shape by means of palm fibers carefully packed together on the face. All the materials covering the body were tied up tightly with a sort of multicolored braid making geometrical patterns.[2] The wealth and great number of garments clothing the dead bear witness to a practice common not only to most Egyptian necropolises (Bawit, Antinoopolis, Karara, Aswan, Akhmin, etc.), but spread through-

Preceding pages:

Square with female bust
Tapestry. Linen and wool
9th century
22 x 19.5 cm
Paris, Musée du Louvre,
Department of Egyptian
Antiquities; inv. AF 6254
This square is part of a
series of heads or "portraits"
whose stylistic evolution can
be traced throughout the
Coptic period.

Fragment of a tunic
Tapestry and tabby. Wool
9th century?
53.5 x 70.5 cm
Paris, Musée du Louvre,
Department of Egyptian
Antiquities; inv. 5940
Animals alternate with
Coptic crosses in a
geometric network.
The lattice effect visible on
one side of the tunic,
indicates that bands were
used to attach the garment
to the body.

14

out the Mediterranean world. The custom was denounced by 4th century clerics such as St. Jerome, St Ambrose and St. Basil.[3]

Reports of archeological digs describing the state of the tombs at the moment of their discovery leave the reader at once amazed and full of wonder at the care taken over the funerary toilet and the attention paid to the least detail of clothing and furniture :

"Woman's costume. Fragment of a shirt of linen muslin, embroidered with blue dots and white hearts. Dress of yellow goffered seersucker with a square neck opening; collar and neckline trimmed with blue braid, brocaded with yellow motifs; insertion down the chest and medallions along the shoulders woven level with the material of the dress; green background with yellow geometric network. Around the hem of the dress, medallions identical to those on the epaulettes, starred octagons on a lozenge grid background. The bottom of the skirt is edged with braid identical to that round the neck. Coat fragment, red floss silk wadding, edged with yellow, green and red fringe.

White and red padded collar.

Hair-curlers to give volume to the hair.

Fragment of a bonnet, red and blue stripes on a brown background. Cord headband, red and yellow chenille. Wooden comb. Red leather shoes with gold leather appliqués edged in blue leather with embossed gilding."[4]

Death for the believer was not an end, but a preparation for a new birth. This may help to understand why the Christians wished to present themselves in their finest clothes at the moment of the resurrection of the body.

It explains, too, why most of the fabrics which have come down to us are only fragments of clothing. They are rarely complete because of the decomposition of the bodies. For this reason, archeologists and collectors have usually cut out the parts with woven decoration to separate them from the often stained and damaged linen cloth. Many Coptic fabrics are thus to be found taken out of context and presented as pictures in museums and private interiors —witness, if any were needed, to the esthetic attraction of these objects.

A DISCOVERY BECOME A FASHION

When the collector and orientalist Emile Guimet asked Albert Gayet to begin excavations on the site of Antinoopolis in the winter of 1896, he had little idea of the wealth of material which would be found there. Of course, many museums had already begun to put together collections of late Egyptian relics, but Gayet's excavations brought to light an artistic genre whose very existence had not been suspected. "Mr. Gayet had come upon archeological deposits of the highest importance, revealing four successive civilizations over a period of five or six centuries. In the fourteen years he has been working there, he has unearthed pieces which are historical documents of the utmost importance for the study of religions, art and social practices. And he has found them in such abundance that all the museums of Europe and France have been supplied" (Emile Guimet). At the Orléans museum, for example, the public "flocked to the exhibition and lectures organized by the Archeological Society in the pretty conference hall [...]. It was the fabrics, tapestries and embroideries which captured everyone's attention.

After a moment of surprise and disappointment at the ruined state of the clothes, the archeologist's imagination soon cast its spell over the lay public, bringing the past to life for them as never before. Having the pieces before their eyes made people understand how much more could be learned from them about the shape of the garments than from ancient statues, and about their colors than from the paintings and mosaics in Ravenna and Rome or from medieval minatures. So much so, indeed, that doubts were expressed about the diversity of weav-

Square with a hare
Tapestry. Wool
6th century
18 x 20 cm
Lyon, Musée Historique des Tissus; inv. 24409
The garland framing the hare is treated in flat tones while the animal itself is given relief by the use of hatching. Animals gleaning fruit are frequent themes in all mediums of Roman art.

ing methods and colors so fresh that the great age of these scraps seemed scarcely credible. Pictures were examined, figures identified, symbols explained. People stopped in front of the Christian tunic, admired the Tree of Paradise and the tapestry flowers, loved Cupid playing the flute, and smiled at the legend of Saint George, protector of virtuous ladies. Fabrics were compared –here was the ancestor of the terry towel!– and many different stitches could be recognized, from Aubusson and Beauvais to Gobelins and Flanders verdure. Memories of Homeric Penelopes and Roman matrons attached to hearth and spindle were revived by the effects of the women of Antinoopolis like Euphemia, buried with her embroidery hoop, ivory boxes, needles and shuttles. The public came to respect these artists and linked modern art to theirs through the Renaissance and byzantium, and through them to the earliest Asiatic centers of civilization."[6]

Soon, ladies were being encouraged to adopt Coptic designs for their home embroidery. The D.M.C. Collection brought out three fascicules by Thérèse de Dillmont (of the Comptoir Alsacien de Broderie in Mulhouse, Alsace) entitled "Motifs de broderie copte, L'art chrétien en Egypte".[7] These offered customers a choice of motifs to embroider using D.M.C. brand cotton, linen and silk products : "The general interest aroused by these discoveries and the novelty and great variety of the embroideries have persuaded us to publish a collection of designs. They present endless possibilities for embroidery subjects, simple to execute and with all the prestige of the original."[8] We should note in passing that Thérèse de Dillmont speaks of "embroideries," whereas Edouard Gerspach, the Administrator of the Gobelins Tapestries, had already observed in 1887 that the fabrics acquired by the Gobelins (some of which came from excavations by Gaston Maspero at Akhmim) had been made on vertical looms, not fundamentally different from those at the Gobelins itself, whence the name "Gobelins coptes" which had quickly been given to them : "Egyptian and Gobelins" fabrics result from methods so nearly identical, apart from certain secondary details, that I was able to have pupils copy them without difficulty."[9]

The idea of reproducing ancient clothes had already been put into practice by Albert Gayet himself in a very striking way. At one of his lectures, two music hall performers showed them off : "I recently saw a delightful traveling coat. It was in russet-colored wool with a sprinkling of pale blue and garnet decorations. Its shape was most singular, being chiefly composed of one large rectangular piece of cloth. The sleeves, very wide, were sewn on with straight stitching. A white braid belt tied in a knot pulled the

Orbiculus with *putti*
Tapestry. Linen and wool
7th century
9 x 7.5 cm
Paris, Musée du Louvre,
Department of Egyptian
Antiquities; inv. AF 5444

The figures in this *orbiculus* represent the end of summer and harvest; one carries an ear of corn and a bunch of grapes, another a sickle and bunch of grapes, the third carries a bird and the fourth, a basket.

Square with foliage scrolls
Tapestry. linen and wool
Akhmin, 6th century
25.5 x 24.1 cm
Paris, Musée du Louvre,
Department of Egyptian
Antiquities; inv. E 10131
The naturalistic treatment of the foliage in this square links it to mosaics of the same period.

folds into harmonious lines. There were no accessories, no collar, tapering or metal buttons; nothing but many-colored motifs in soft, muted tones which formed a succession of triangles falling from the neckline down the back and chest, and rising from the botton of the garment towards the middle of the legs. Where did I see such a coat? Not at the races or on top of a mail-coach or at the station; it was simply the garment of a young woman from Antinoopolis in about the year 400 A.D. worn by two pretty Parisians in the year 1903 for the pleasure of our eyes and imaginations, and for the satisfaction of Mr. Gayet, explorer of genius and Byzantine fashion designer."[10]

In his lecture, Albert Gayet evoked the magnificence of the fabrics he had discovered with the grandiloquence typical of turn-of-the-century orators: "Look at them! Heavy and dull after seventeen centuries of darkness, yellowed and charged with the long, slow exhalation of incense and spices, these fabrics still blaze with light and life! Imagine the luster and fire with which these tunics and robes, these mantles and shawls, must have shone forth in roads and busy marketplaces when the sun, glancing off shoulders and hips, lit up their sparkling colors, breathing life into the Cupids and Bacchants, the Apollos and Venuses, the birds, flowers and medallions, and making the blood of Tyrian purples shimmer from shoulders to feet at the slightest movement..."[11]

In 1898, in a more sober vein, he indicated very accurately the essential role that these discoveries would henceforth play in historical study: "Up to now, these styles, fabrics and silk appliqués, whether Roman or Byzantine, have only been known to us in representation: the sculptures in Salonica, the frescos of Saint Vitus and Saint Apollinarius in Ravenna, manuscript miniatures. Their interest is thus far greater than that of the rest of our discoveries, both for the history of clothing in Antiquity and for that of weaving techniques used at the time."[12]

Albert Gayet's enthusiasm led him to make use of pieces of cloth and other objects as decorations for two books. The first contained two illustrated works by him: *Antinoé et les sépultures de Thaïs et Sérapion* (Paris, Société Française d'Edition, 1912), and *Fantomes d'Antinoé —Les sépultures de Leukyoné et Myrithis* (Paris, 1904). The front cover, lining and endpapers are covered with tapestries. The second volume contains 24 pieces of cloth on a background of white paper. The covers, linings and endpapers have the same type of decoration as the preceding volume. Furthermore, at the end of the album, the binding is hollowed out to contain all kinds of different objects: pieces of cloth, leather, ivory, wood,

glass, etc.[13] (These collections, which came up for sale in 1928, now belong to the Henry Art Gallery of the University of Washington).

The discoveries at Antinoopolis had an impact hard to imagine today: "These costumes particularly interested the Parisians. Mr. Thomas, the wardrobe master at the Opera obtained permission to draw them and made models of these Byzantine costumes, reproducing the different ornaments. With these it was possible to mount a new staging of "Theodora." The costumes of the chorus and all the actors were remade from the designs."

Two operas with the name of "Theodora" date from this period, one by Jules Massenet (1842-1912), the other by Xavier Leroux (1863-1919). Unfortunately it is impossible to identify which one Mr. Thomas worked for. We still have this precious account, however, which continues in these terms: "Mr. Thomas had been so struck by the interest of these finds that he thought of displaying them in the Palais du Costume, and it was he, with several friends, who carried out the third year of excavations entirely at their own expense."

Since the beginning of this century, the attraction of modern painters for "exotic" civilizations has led some of them to take an interest in Coptic art, and particularly the fabrics, whose inspiration they seemed to share: "Matisse's affinity with Coptic art can be most strongly felt in works from his Fauvist period: his art and theirs are both the fruit of a violent and dynamic distortion of one aesthetic system by another, whose structures gradually emerge in the dismembering of the first, above all by the use of pure color. However, this affinity can be felt in later periods too. With their deliberate awkwardness and "childlikeness," the vegetable, animal, architectural and geometrical motifs in the great gouache cut-outs of the last period, still suggest Coptic fabrics. Finally, when one remembers that most of the Coptic weaving that has come down to us is from liturgical garments, one cannot help recognizing in the chasubles designed by Matisse for the officiants of his Chapel, a last echo of the impression made on him at the outset of his career by the dalmatics which Georges Duthuit, in 1927, described in terms that apply perfectly to the fabrics of 1950.[14]"

Henri Matisse's (1869-1954) interest in Coptic fabrics came from direct acquaintance. He had a small

Pan and Dionysus
Tapestry. Wool
5-7th centuries
40 x 36 cm
Boston, Museum of Fine Arts;
inv. 53.18
This static and stylized
scene depicts the well-
known episode of the
drunken Dionysus supported
by Pan or Silenus. In the
background are amphora,
crotala and panpipes, objects
associated with the cult of
Dionysus.

examples. This interest continued thoughout his life. In 1932 he wrote to a friend : "I have found the Coptic tapestry which I talked about to Mr. Hanotaux. I've enclosed three photos of the eagle cloth- as well as the one of the reliquary in the Louvre."[15]

Matisse, therefore, along with other painters who came out of Fauvism, was particularly sensitive to the forms and colors created by these remote ancestors of modern weavers. Pierre Schneider analyzes the relation between Matisse and Coptic tapestries thus : "It was natural that Matisse should have felt a particular affinity for the art of the Copts, for their situation had been comparable to his. They were faced with the task not of rejecting but of remodeling the Hellenistic heritage in order to adapt it to an aesthetic that was as far removed from the Greco-Latin tradition as the mythological repertory they drew on was from the Christian vision to which they had to subordinate it. The solution emerged from the stylistic conflict itself : the classical image is kneaded and dynamized by the play of conflicting forces. Proportion is discarded in favor of expressive distortion. Delicate harmonies and subtle transitions cannot survive such aggression : all that remains is the general outline, simplified masses, sharply contrasted spaces and solids, rough contours, and a few bright tones. 'With the Copts we are at the sources of color', wrote Georges Duthuit. "Our generation

collection, now in the possession of Mr Claude Duthuit, the painter's heir. "East and West, surface and depth, confront each other in Coptic fabrics, as in the work of Matisse himself. He was passionately interested in them from the beginning of the century, according to Georges Duthuit, the painter's son-in-law and a great connoisseur of the art. He probably discovered them at the 1900 Paris World's Fair, where the Coptic tapestries unearthed by Albert Gayet at Antinoopolis had attracted a great deal of attention. The Louvre and the Musée Guimet offered him other

has nothing to lose by coming to them to quench its thirst." Matisse did not fail to do so, but in addition to his feeling for color –the great lesson of the Orient as a whole– he was sensitive to the particularities of Coptic art. The message of Islamic rugs hardly differed from that of Coptic fabrics, but its studied refinement had less to say to turn-of-the century Western artists, infatuated with primitivism and dreaming of violent shocks and breaks, than the rough innocence and fresh intensity of this folk art. The relationship of Coptic textiles to Oriental rugs is rather like that of the highly colored "cheap prints" of Japanese woodcuts to their less forceful, more "distinguished" originals. As we have seen, Matisse preferred the first.[16]"

An American contemporary of Matisse, the painter Marsden Hartley (1877-1943), was strongly attracted at the end of his life by the portraits of the Fayum* and Coptic textiles, which for him represented the genius of Antiquity. In the catalog of an exhibition of his paintings in 1941 : he wrote : "I must not forget to speak of the Coptic embroideries, which, for me are classics in great painting, because they must basically have been great painters who made them.

I think I was never more completely bowled over than when I saw the amazing collection of these embroideries which were recently shown by my friend Mr. Dikran Kelekian, who after possessing them for forty years, decided to show them at last, of which I am now the possessor of five examples, and when I want to know about great tonality, I get them out like a pack of cards and play a sort of solitaire.[17]"

1. H.E. WINLOCK and W.E. CRUM, 1926, part I, p. 48-50, pl. XI-XII.
2. Jean CLEDAT, D.A.C.L., II, 1, col. 215.
3. H. LECLERCQ, D.A.C.L., XV, 2, col. 2411-2412.
4. Albert GAYET, 1898, p. 31-32.
5. Emile GUIMET, 1913, p. 4.
6. Jules BAILLET, 1907, p. 3-4.
7. Thérèse de DILLMONT, 3 fascules, not dated.
8. Thérèse de DILLMONT, First fascicule, p. 3.
9. Edouard GERSPACH, 1890.
10. Maurice RAVIDOUT, *Fémina*, p. 621-622.
11. Maurice RAVIDOUT, *Fémina*, p. 622.
12. Albert GAYET, 1898, p. 13.
13. *Catalogue des livres d'heures enluminés...*, 1928, nº 26.
14. Pierre SCHNEIDER, 1984, p. 170.
15. Pierre SCHNEIDER, 1984, p. 168.
16. Pierre SCHNEIDER, 1984, p. 168.
17. *Cincinnati Modern Art Society*, 1941, p. 4-6.

FROM
THREAD
TO LOOM

MAKING THE CLOTH

The fibers

Coptic textiles usually have a warp of unbleached linen and a woof of dyed wool in decorated parts. The grounding for these is most often in unbleached linen, though dyeing becomes somewhat commoner towards the end of the period.

The use of flax was an ancient tradition in Egypt; largescale production dates back at least to the beginning of the historical period (c.3100 B.C.). The flax was harvested at different stages of its growth, depending on what it was intended for. The green stems had soft fibers, yielding the fine thread needed for the cloth which would cover mummies and the statues of gods, and which the Greeks called byssos; the coarser-fibered yellow stems served to make thicker, warmer clothes; and the tough fibers of very ripe stems were used in rope and matting. These different grades of thread can be clearly seen in Coptic fabrics; indeed, their texture is largely due to the initial choice of fiber. Pliny the Edler *(Natural History,* XIX, 16-18) describes in detail the different stages in the cultivation and dressing of flax. After being tied up in sheaves and dried in the sun, the stems were combed out with a wood or metal comb to remove the seeds (rippling); then they were left to soak in water to isolate the fibers (retting); after this they were broken and finally separated with a comb (carding). The fibers thus obtained were reformed into bundles or balls and placed in baskets or earthenware pots which the spinner could easily manipulate. Distaffs were also used from the Greco-Roman period. They were usually made of a reed with one end split into several strips to which the bundle of flax to be spun was attached.[1]

Wool being perishable, little has been discovered in tombs from the age of the Pharaohs. The ancient Egyptians no doubt used the wool from the great flocks of sheep so often depicted in their tombs, but it was not until the Greek period (from 332 B.C.) that wool was produced on a large scale and it never replaced flax, which long remained the Egyptian national fiber. Herodotus *(Histories,* II, 81) says that religious law forbade wool in tombs and sanctuaries because of its animal origin. This aversion must have disappeared under the Romans and Christians, as tombs from this period have yielded thousands of decorated fabrics in flax and wool.

No written account of the preparation of wool in Egypt has come down to us; however the process was undoubtedly the same as in other Mediterranean countries: after shearing, the wool was washed,

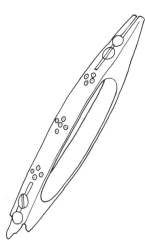

Reed distaff

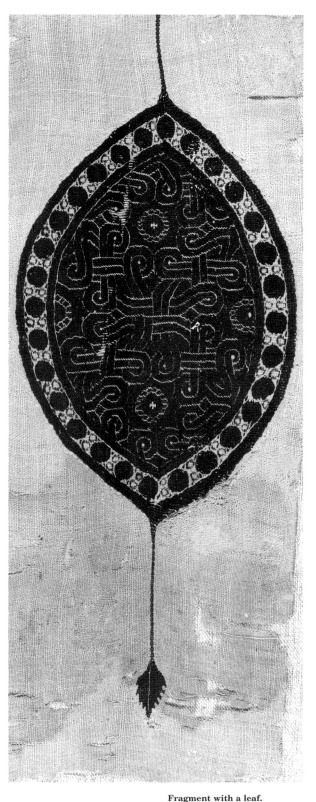

Fragment with a leaf.
Tapestry and tabby. Linen and
wool
4-5th centuries
33.3 x 14 cm
Paris, Musée du Louvre,
Department of Antiquities ;
inv. AF 5884
The purple-violet leaf is
covered with a network of
interlaces executed by a
flying shuttle.

24

beaten to remove the impurities and then carded.

The discovery of silk in large quantities in the necropolises of Akhmin and Antinopolis presents us with problem of its origin. The pieces are all in the Sassanid* style, suggesting that many may have been imported already finished. Other historical evidence supports this, for until the Arab conquest (641 A.D.), silk coming from the Far East passed through Persia, which was an important trading center, first under the Parthians then under the Sassanids. Here, Mediterranean products met others coming from the Far East. We know that Egyptian woolworkers skilfully adapted Sassanid themes and compositions, but it seems very unlikely that they wove the silk discovered at Akhmin and Antinopolis themselves. On the other hand, mixed silk can be recognized in the weft of certain Coptic fabrics, and we know from the Theodosian Code (438 A.D.) that there was a "gynaeceum" in Alexandria producing silk goods for the Imperial court which was as renowned as the workshops of Byzantium itself or the great cities of the East, Damascus, Antioch, Tyre or Sidon. Towards the middle of the 6th century, the introduction of silkworm eggs broke the Persian monopoly and led to the development of a flourishing industry related to the luxurious Byzantine court life. No doubt it was Imperial officers and functionaries who had brought silk to Egypt at the beginning of the 5th century.[2]

Silk is much simpler to prepare than other textile fibers. After being plunged in boiling water, the cocoon is unwound in one continuous thread which can be woven without needing to be spun. Similarly, several threads can be twisted together to make a thicker, tougher thread.

Wild tusser-silk was used in an unusual way - for the warp and trimming - on a unique piece of Coptic fabric dating from the 6th century: a piece of galloon decorated with vine foliage in which stands a putto holding a cloth filled with flowers and fruit (Musée Historique des Tissus, Lyon n°38.845).[3]

Cotton, originally from India, does not seem to have been much used in Egypt. Herodotus mentions it (III,47): the "breastplate" of the 26th dynasty king Amasis was made of "tree wool", he says. And Pliny reports that Egyptian priests had a liking for cotton clothes (Natural History, XIX,14). Cotton fabrics have been discovered at Meroé in the Sudan an Karanog in Nubia; these are the earliest known from the Greco-Roman period. And an inscription from about 350 A.D. tells us that cotton was stored in Nubia - perhaps for export to Egypt.[4] But in spite of all this, and the discovery of cotton samples in the monastery of Saint Phoebammon near Thebes (4th century A.D.), the cultivation and use of cotton seem only to have reached Egypt after the arrival of the Arabs.[5] No cotton fabric of Coptic manufacture has been dated earlier than that.

Gold thread was used by the Copts to enhance the precious character of certain fabrics. The linen, silk and, later, cotton threads were wrapped in with strips of beaten gold. There are numerous ancient accounts of the custom of gilding cloth, but unfortunately, very little of the material has survived. Besides Egypt, remains have been brought to light in the Near East, where this technique seems to have originated; and fragments from the Roman period have been discovered further afield, in Hungary and France.[6]

Spinning

This included all the operations -stretching, twisting and winding- involved in making thread out of the separate fibers. None of these required tools: the fibers could simply be rolled together between the finger and thumb or the palms of the hands or, more often, between the palm and the thigh, so as to leave a hand free to draw the fibers out before twisting. However, it was much more usual to use a wooden spindle loaded with one or two whorls to give it momentum and to provide a hook for the yarn. These spindle-whorls might be in wood, stone, bronze, ivory or even terracotta. Turning the spindle twisted the fibers together into a single strand which was wrapped round the stem when it became too long to handle easily.[7] When no more yarn would fit on the spindle, it was formed into a skein or used directly for warping. The most skilful spinners could work two spindles at once (a Coptic text records that a certain David had spun 48 threads with each pair of spindles). Warp thread, needing to be stronger than the woof, had to be twisted more, and in the great textile centers these two kinds of yarn were often spun by separate specialists.

Dressing the fibers and spinning were household tasks. A large number of spindles, some with the remains of wool or linen threads still round them, have been unearthed in urban sites, necropolises and monasteries.

In Egyptian villages today, as in Antiquity, one can still see peasant women twirling spindles as they gossip on their doorsteps. Like knitting, it is a simple activity which does not require any particular attention and allows one to do "two things at once". This is why monks and ascetics very often spun; it left them free in their minds to pray or recite passages of Scripture as they worked.

In 1950, a study of thread twist was carried out by the Textile Museum in Washington D.C. It analyzed

Wooden spindle

the museum's own collection as well as important groups in other American museums and at the Victoria and Albert Museum in London.[9] It seems that flax naturally twists to the left in an "S" as it dries; as a result, says the study, in Egypt linen was spun this way from the earliest times, and a leftward twist is to be found in all Egyptian cloth. Fifteen years earlier, Rodolphe Pfister noted that "all the Egyptian Gobelins that we have been able to examine (and which in fact almost all come from Antinopolis) present a leftward twist. A rightward twist is an argument for a foreign origin".[10]

In fact, however, this one technical criterion is not enough to identify a fabric's origin. A large number of specimens, from the Orient as well as from Egypt, present both ways of spinning.

Dyeing

Wool was dyed before spun, linen and cotton before being woven. Finished garments were rarely dyed, although white clothes were washed and bleached to finish. While dressing the fibers, spinning and weaving were household tasks, fulling, bleaching, scouring and dyeing were very delicate procedures, carried out in special workshops. Only two such establishments have been found in Egypt, a fulling mill at Tebtunis in the Fayum, and a dyeworks at Athribis in the Delta, where tanks still survive bearing traces of blue and red dye.[11] In an article published in 1935,[12] the chemist Rodolphe Pfister presented the results of his research on Oriental

dyestuffs, based on the analysis of fabrics from Egypt and Syria. He also compared traditional dyeing methods with those mentioned in three ancient collections containing recipes for dyeing wool: the Greek-language *Papyrus x* in the Leyden museum (end of the 3rd-4th century A.D.), one of a series of twenty-four papyri bought in 1829 by the Dutch government from I. Anastasy, the Swedish consul in Alexandria; the *Papyrus Graecus Holmiensis* dating from the same period, and presented to the Stockholm Academy in 1832 by the same consul; and lastly, *Physica et Mystica*, a work by Bolos Democritos of Mendes in the Delta, who lived in Alexandria around the year 200 B.C., although the oldest copy of his work, conserved in Library of Saint Mark's in Venice, dates from the end of the 10th century.

Pfister's analyses were based on chemical tests and are not always reliable. However, he was the first in this field to demonstrate the importance of the study of techniques, and since his pioneering research, workers in several countries have used spectrotophometry and chromatography -which only need to remove tiny samples- on ancient fabrics. Since 1984 for example, the Textile Section of the French *Monuments Historiques* research laboratory at Champs-sur-Marne has undertaken a systematic analysis of the fibers, dyes and fixatives in the Louvre's collection of Coptic fabrics.[13]

Washing the thread always came before any other operation. Wool in particular was impregnated with greasy substances and had to be cleaned with detergents such as cinders, natron (a hydrated carbonate of sodium found on some lake borders), or potash, alkaline plants like soapwort and asphodel, or fermented urine, which contained ammonia.

After washing came the use of mordants, an important and difficult stage because the final nuances of color depended on the initial choice of mordants and the way it was applied. Without mordants the dyes would not penetrate to the heart of the fibers. The agent most commonly employed in Antiquity was alum, a double salt of aluminum and potassium, but the salts of iron, chrome and tin were also used. As we have seen, only the woof was dyed in Coptic fabrics. This was made of wool, which, unlike linen, dyes very well, and for this reason was used on a large scale in decorated fabrics from the Greco-Roman period on.

The dyes were of animal or vegetable origin. High-priced foreign dyestuffs, like cochineal from Armenia or kermes from Asia Minor, were little used in Egypt. The best dyes were probably reserved for dyers in the big towns.

Pliny the Elder mentions an Egyptian technique

of printing on linen cloth (*Natural History*, XXXV, 42) although the only examples we have of this date from the 4th century A.D. and later. First, the dyer spread a protective layer of wax or clay on the parts not to be dyed; then he applied a mordant . After this, the cloth was plunged into a bath of dye, usually indigo. Some of these fabrics, due perhaps to ageing, are now green; others are red, as the result of an appropriate mordant. The dye was sometimes applied with brushes or wood-stamps. The most famous example of this technique is the "Antinoopolis veil" in the Louvre; but the Abegg Foundation in Riggisberg near Bern also has a large printed hanging representing Artemis accompanied by mythological heroes.[14] Fabric printing, till the 7th century chiefly used to illustrate scenes from the Old and New Testaments, continued in the Arab period for decorating clothes.

Starting with primary colors (red, blue and yellow), all the other colors could be obtained, along with their nuances:

- Red: this was the color most frequently used in Antiquity because of its great resistance. It was chiefly obtained from the root of madder *(Rubia tinctorium)*, a plant first used for dyeing by the Egyptians. Diluted, it gives varieties of pink. Archil *(Roccella)*, a lichen found on rocky coasts in the Eastern Mediterranean, was also apparently used.

Red was also obtained from the kermes, an insect found in the kermes oak *(Quercus coccifera)* which grows on the Mediterranean coast and in the Middle East. The dye was obtained from the eggs. The cochineal, an insect of the same family as the kermes *(Coccidae)*, had to be imported from Armenia. It was replaced by lac-dye, a dark-red resin produced on the twigs of trees in India by another insect of the same family. The appearance of this dye in Egypt corresponds to the breaking of relations with Armenia, Byzantium and the North after the Arab invasion in the middle of the 7th century. The presence or absence of this dyestuff thus provides a way of dating Coptic fabrics in this period. Rodolphe Pfister notes however that "lac-dye, a coloring agent produced by an Indian insect, *coccus lacca*, was certainly known in Egypt in the first century A.D.; it is mentioned in the *Voyage round the Erythrean Sea* as being brought from India.[15]

- Blue: this was obtained by soaking the leaves of the indigo plant, *Indigofera tinctorea*, imported from India, or *Indigofera argentea*, which grows wild in Nubia, Kordofan*, Sennar* and Abyssinia*. Blue was also obtained from woad, which seems to have been cultivated in the Fayum in the Christian era.

- Purple: this can be anything from a wine-colored red-violet through brown-violet to an almost black violet-blue. Up till now, no genuine purple -a dyes-

tuff extracted from the shellfish, murex brandaris- has been found in any Coptic fabric. However, Pfister claims to have detected it in 3rd century fabrics discovered at Palmyra. Obtaining purple from the murex was a complicated and costly business, and dyers made do with substitutes such as kermes and archil. The most common technique, and one we find constantly in Coptic fabrics, consisted in combining madder and indigo.

- Yellow: this was nearly all obtained from plants like weld, saffron and pomegranate flowers. Weld or dyer's rocket is the commonest of these in Coptic fabrics. Depending on the mordant used, different nuances of yellow and orange could be obtained. Unfortunately, these colors are far less resistant, and easily lose their brilliance and intensity.

"To sum up, all the substances which provided colors for the skilful Coptic dyers have an organic origin. Their resistance is remarkable, at least as good as that of the best Gobelins colors. The Coptic tapestries in our museum have been brought from a land of blazing sunshine, and after a long period underground, which no doubt preserved them, they have again been exposed to the sun for a time sufficiently long for the experiment to be conclusive: the colors have resisted so well that one might think they had just come out of the workshop."[16]

The looms

As soon as the thread was ready, warping could begin. The warp was prepared either with pegs on the wall or with posts in the ground, and then mounted on the loom. No loom has yet been discovered, as they were made of wood and so were easily taken to pieces and transported; furthermore, wood was relatively rare in Egypt and would be reused, often ending up in the fire. However, weaving techniques have not changed, and we have wooden models dating from the Middle Kingdom, paintings from the Age of Pharaohs, and evidence of weaving methods in the cloth and tapestries which have been brought to light. In addition, numerous articles connected with weaving were placed in the tombs, a custom found in other civilizations as well. Out of this amazingly well-preserved Egyptian material, we can reconstruct complete weaving "kits", so to speak, providing a context which breathes new life into such objects as the "little embroidery box" (actually, its contents seem better suited for spinning and weaving) discovered by Albert Gayet in a woman's tomb in Antinopolis: "This *nécessaire* contains an embroidery hoop with pegs to attach the cloth; a distaff; an ivory case; a comb to bring the threads closer together; some spindles loaded with wool; a reel; a reed case with two compartments containing needles; some wooden and ivory needles to separate the threads; some reed needles, flattened at the tip and with wool and silk attached; a box containing a resinous substance; a little ivory casket subdivided into four compartments; and a whole set of square pieces of sycamore wood, with a hole pierced in each of the four corners, whose function is difficult to determine at the moment."[17]

Several types of looms are known to have existed in Egypt. The oldest, the horizontal (or low-warp) loom, goes back to the Neolithic period; it was the sole loom until the end of the Middle Kingdom (c. 1570 B.C.), but was used only sporadically after that. The vertical (or high-warp) loom, no doubt invented in Syria or Palestine, was introduced at the beginning of the New Kingdom, when Egypt was acquiring an Empire in the Orient, and its adoption coincides with the appearance of decorated clothes showing an oriental influence in their techniques of manufacture. It is very likely that the majority of Coptic textiles were woven on vertical looms, which are easier to manipulate than horizontal ones, the cloth being woven from the bottom to the top. However, an improved version of the horizontal loom, probably also originating in the Orient, appeared in Alexandria in the 1st century A.D. Archaeologists excavating the monastery of Saint Epiphanius at Thebes claim to have recognized the site of nine pedal-looms dating from the 7th century A.D.[18] These are horizontal looms with heddles -that is, vertical cords with loops to receive the warp-threads- suspended from a harness and worked by pedals, thus freeing the weaver's hands from having to lift the warp-threads all the time. On these relatively elaborate looms, simple decorated fabrics were woven.

One kind of vertical loom used weights made of stone or clay to stretch the warp; weaving went from top to bottom. Weights apparently dating from the New Kingdom have been discovered in Middle Egypt, and this loom was the only one used by the Greeks.

During the Roman period, Alexandria was particularly renowned for its *polymita*, complex weaves for decorated fabrics which required special looms. "But it was Alexandria which began weaving what are called *Polymita*, using a large number of heddles" (Pliny, *Natural History*, VIII, 74,2). Weaving errors in certain 3rd and 4th century decorated fabrics from Antinopolis show that a horizontal loom was in use with an independent system for lifting the warp-threads. This was worked from outside the loom by strings attached to one of the sides of the frame. This loom permitted the manufacture of complex fabrics with coherent patterns or repeated motifs, some with "no underside".

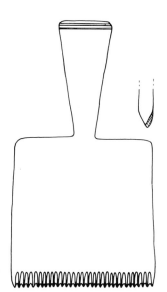

Wooden weaver's comb

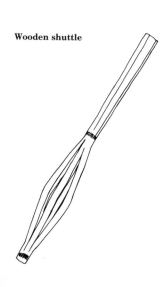

Wooden shuttle

Galloons, for sewing onto garments, and belts were often woven on so-called "card" or "tablet" looms. The warp-threads, in dyed wool, went through holes pierced in little tablets made of bone, wood, leather or card. To make a piece of braid, a certain number of tablets -from ten to a hundred- had to be associated. Each turn of the plates created a gap into which the unbleached linen woof-thread was fed. This kept in place the intertwined warp-threads forming the pattern, while remaining invisible. The most ancient known specimen of this was found at Thebes (New Kingdom), but the most famous example is the "belt of Ramses III" in Liverpool.[20]

This is the function of the small square tablets with round holes at the corners discovered at Antinopolis which Albert Gayet was unable to explain.[21] The Royal Museums of Art and History in Brussels possess twenty-five "tablets" from the tomb of the embroideress Euphemiaan; the Louvre has seventeen examples which also seem to have come from Antinoopolis.

Bags and snoods with a lace-like appearance were made following the technique of *sprang*. This word, of Scandinavian origin, at first designated all loose-textured fabrics; it was later restricted to the plaiting of warp-threads attached at both ends.[22]

Some technical weaving terms and procedures

- Selfbands: several warp-threads are pulled together by woof-thread along their whole length, creating a thick line in matching tones which can be repeated at regular intervals.
- Pulled threads: the woof has temporary interruptions, leaving gaps (openwork borders of shawls).
- Slits: formed by the parallel work of two shuttles. Slits are sometimes left as they are for decorative pruposes. They can also be sewn up, but the seams are fragile and have often disappeared from ancient fabrics. For this reason, the neighboring pieces of cloth are often made to overlap.
- Floating warp: the woof leaves free some of the warp-threads, which "float" on the back of the fabric.
- Floating woof: the unbleached woof hangs loose on the back of the decorative motif.
- Color beating: the alternation of unbleached linen and dyed wool threads, creating a mottled effect.
- Gradation of colors: this consists in weaving in succession several woof-threads of unequal length. The colors interpenetrate and give illusion of relief.
- Flying shuttle: the illusion of relief can be replaced by laying the colors on flat. To draw certain details of the decoration (e.g., facial features, body muscles, the veins of leaves, or geometrical lines),

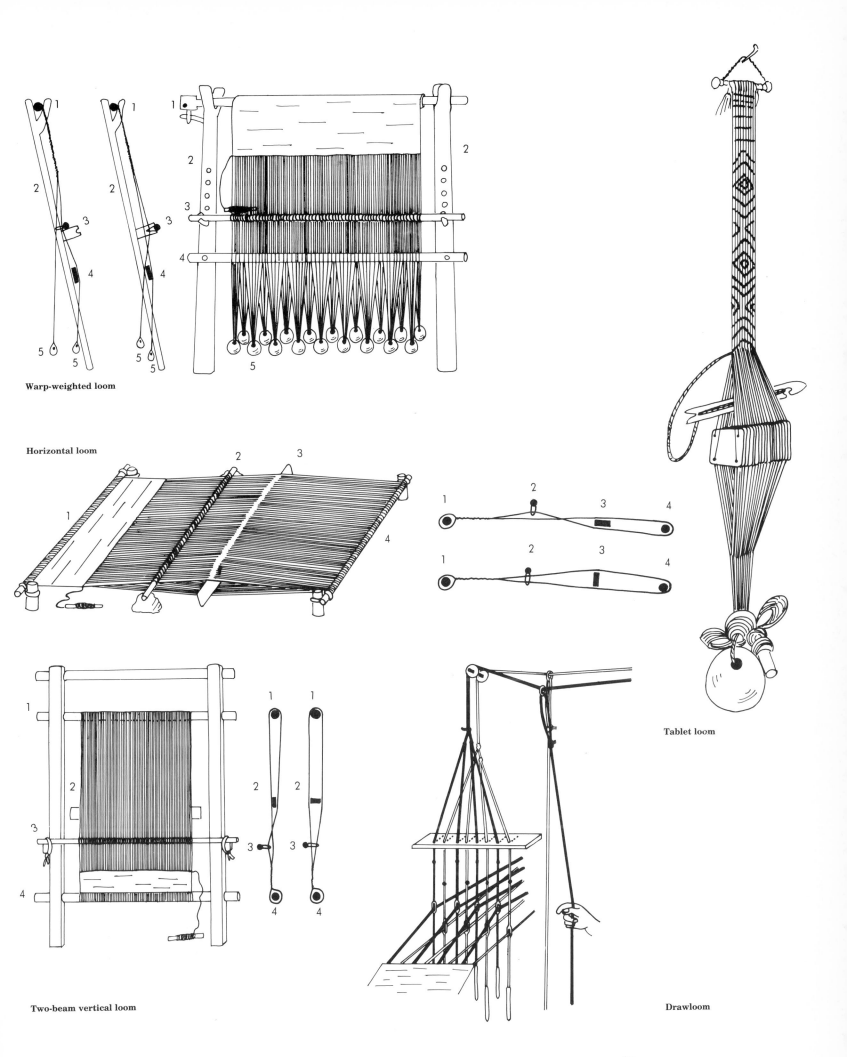

Warp-weighted loom

Horizontal loom

Two-beam vertical loom

Tablet loom

Drawloom

31

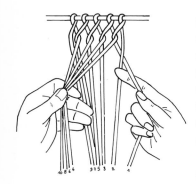

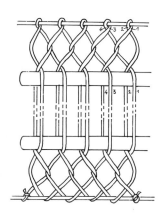

Sprang technique

the weaver uses additional shuttles, often pulling unbleached linen threads, over and above the regular work of the standard shuttle. The flexibility of these shuttles offers the possibility of working in all directions, with continuous curves in the direction of the woof and quantum leaps in the direction of the warp. This procedure, universally used from the 7th century on, is characteristic of Coptic fabrics.

-Brocading: a woof thread, often unbleached, produces geometric motifs using wrapped outlines.

- Bouclé: a woof-thread goes round a small rod at regular intervals, forming loops; these are then kept in place by a thread of unbleached linen and the beating of subsequent woof-threads. This type of fabric is probably of Oriental origin; the oldest known Egyptian example dates from the Middle Kingdom and comes from Deir el Bahari.

Two particular cases: embroidery and knitting

Although they are much rarer, the embroidered fabrics form an ensemble whose interest lies not only in the way they are made, but also in their great iconographical homogeneity.

Wool or, more commonly, silk thread was embroidered on a linen ground. Embroidery probably has an Oriental origin. Embroidered fabrics unearthed in Syria and Mesopotamia go back to the beginning of the 1st millenium B.C. The fabrics from the tomb of Thutmosis IV, some of which belonged to Amenophis II (c. 1439-1413), and the tunic of Tutenkhamen (c.1347-1337) have decorative elements treated in embroidery. The themes used (palm-leaves, a gry-

phon, a winged sphinx with a female head) also suggest a strong Oriental influence. In the same way, the "Coptic" embroidered fabrics, mostly dating from the 5th to the 7th centuries, leave us with the problem of their origin: are these embroideries by Oriental workers settled in Egypt or by Egyptian workers imitating Oriental and Byzantine styles and iconographies.

Coptic wollen knitwear consists of socks and belts in stocking stitch. Knitted pieces are rather rare - perhaps a reflection of the excavators' lack of interest in these insignificant articles of clothing.

THE TEXTILE ECONOMY

The production and trade in raw materials

The most numerous sources of information date from the Hellenistic and Roman periods. In spite of deep transformations in the social structure during the Byzantine and Arab periods, there does not seem to have been any fundamental change in this domain.

Flax cultivation was strictly controlled. Already in the Third Dynasty there was a "Director of all the King's flax". In the Greco-Roman period, the central government fixed each year the number of arures (unit areas of agricultural land) to be sown. The trade, however, seems to have been free.

Over wool production and trade, the royal authority had no monopoly. Only certain foreign wools were subject to a tax of 20%.

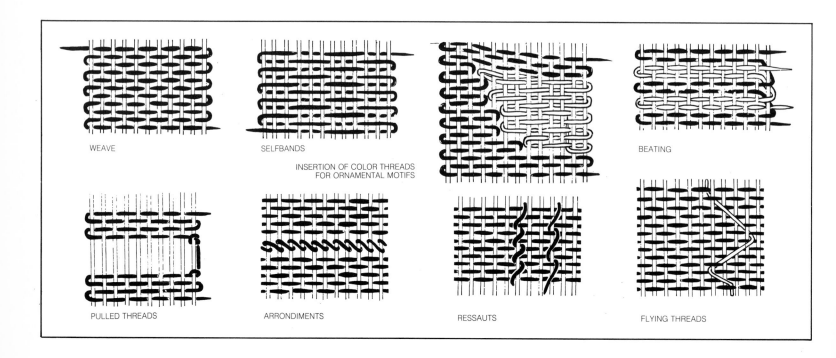

WEAVE

SELFBANDS

INSERTION OF COLOR THREADS
FOR ORNAMENTAL MOTIFS

BEATING

PULLED THREADS

ARRONDIMENTS

RESSAUTS

FLYING THREADS

32

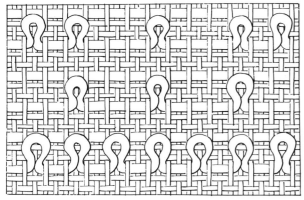

Loop weaving technique

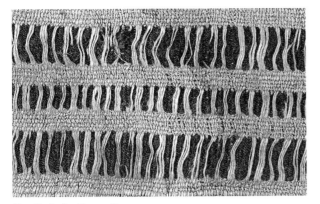

Detail of a floating weft
Tapestry
Linen and wool
Paris, Musée du Louvre,
Department of Egyptian
Antiquities; inv. E 28456
In a floating weft, the
undyed weft passes or
"floats" under the
ornamental motif.

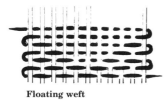

Floating weft

Detail of a tapestry
Linen and wool
9th century
Paris, Musée du Louvre,
Department of Egyptian
Antiquties; inv. AF 5664
Above: Flying shuttle in
chainette stitch. Different
calibers of linen yarn.
Below: Flying shuttle in
which the a thread circles
the same warp thread
between rows of weaving.
Warp slit-formed by the
parallel work of two
shuttles.

33

Tunic with cavaliers
Tapestry and tabby
Linen and wool
Akmin, 7th century
45.5 x 85 cm
Paris, Musée du Louvre, Department of Egyptian Antiquities; inv. E 10130
This tunic is a good example of figurative decoration used on a piece of clothing.
The very refined fabric is heightened
by numerous rows of shaded lines carefully treated by self-bands.

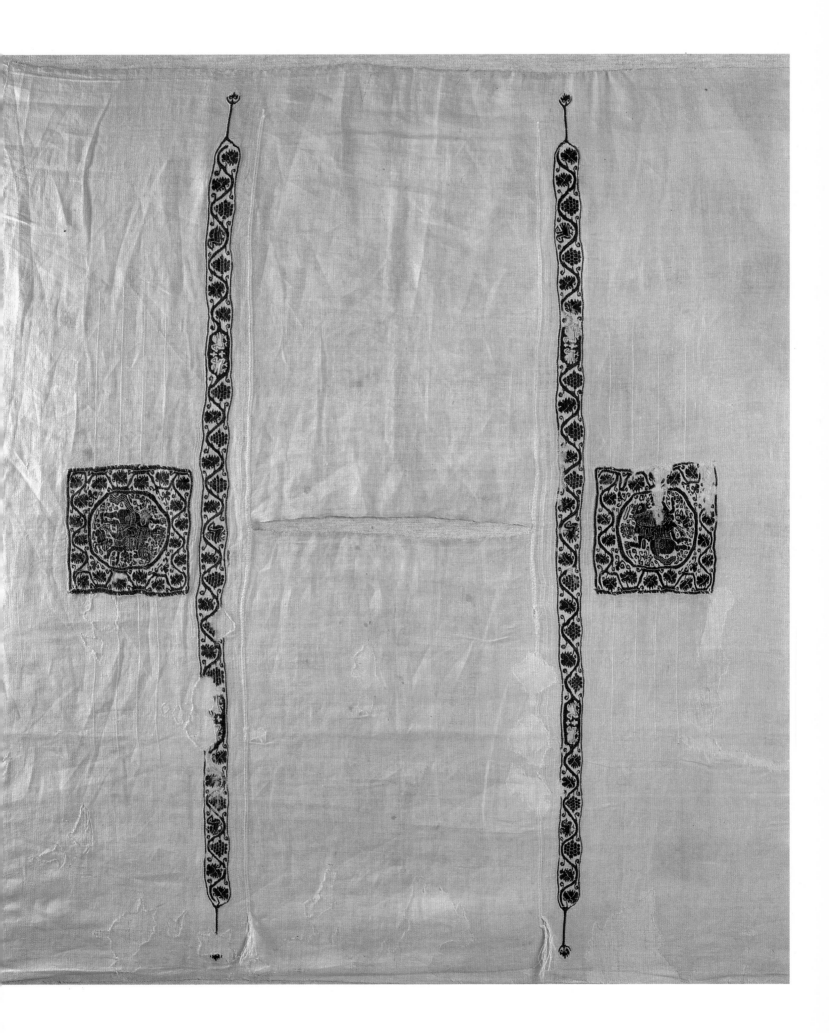

The organization of work

From the time of the Ptolemies, large-scale household production prevailed. The weavers were organized in corporations with a president ("master of the looms") who decided the rules and entered into contact with government officials. Each year the weavers produced a set amount of cloth, prescribed for each nome (region) by the central government. At lower levels the work was distributed to towns and villages, and then to the particular workshops. After a careful inspection by the steward, the weavers were paid according to fixed tariffs which could vary according to the quality and the quantity supplied. Their work – at least the linen goods – was thus, in effect, requisitioned, though wool remained a "free market". Nevertheless, licenses were sometimes granted to certain weavers to sell their products in the markets.

Unused weaving-looms were sealed and placed in reserves in the capital of the nome in order to fight against unauthorized production: "Visit also the workshops where *othonia** are woven and make every effort to see that as many looms as possible are at work and that the weavers produce the contribution of fancy material required of the nome. Those who do not deliver the lengths of cloth required will pay the price, established for each grade by the decree. Sternly demand that the *othonia* be well made and that they have the number of threads required by the regulations..." "Let all the looms which are idle be transported to the metropolis of the nome, gathered in warehouses and sealed" (*Papyrus tebtunis*, 703, 1, 87-117). There were also royal manufactories or *ergasteria*. Temple workshops, however, which produced large amounts of fine linen *(byssus)* to clothe the statues of gods, practically escaped all royal control.

For the Roman period, a thorough study has been made by Ewa Wipszycka, in which she demonstrates that craft activities were free and independent. It was only at the end of the Empire that the principle of the heredity of trades and membership of corporations appeared. During the second half of the 3rd century and the 4th century, the economic structure of Egypt gradually changed with the formation of great landed estates: "In the fourth century, a class of great landowners emerged who, by ceaselessly augmenting their estates at the expense of small tenant farmers, and bringing their free neighbors under their patronage, making clients and settlers of them, had, thanks to "autophagy"*, become more or less independent in their domains. In the 5th and particularly the 6th centuries, these great landlords were very numerous in Egypt, and very powerful.

They formed a kind of feudal nobility..."[24] It was therefore within the framework of great feudal estates that a large amount of all craft activity now took place: "we can, however, assume that there was a development, going from a relatively free work contract to the loss of independence by the worker and his attachment to the domain."[25]

The State manufactories survived under the name of "gyneceum", which originally meant "the part of the house reserved for the women, where the servants would spin, weave and embroider, thus forming a veritable workshop". The manufactory had at its head a high-ranking functionary who depended on the "account of sacred liberalities." The monasteries also had their own weaving looms: at Deir el Medineh, instructions were written on the wall for the weavers and tailors;[26] a papyrus fragment recounting the life of the apa* Bgoul describes the setting up of a loom in the monastery founded by the apa: "one of the brothers, named Martis, having seen that they had multiplied and that they sorely lacked clothes, approached him (Bgoul) and exhorted him to build a weaving shop so that he could make the tunics they needed, for it was his trade."[27]

In the Arab period, we find the same organization, with the "tiraz" (a word of Persian origin meaning embroidery). this was a government workshop in which the textiles needed by the State, the Caliph and the Sultan were made. Public workshops also existed, but these were heavily taxed.

In addition to supplying national needs, a good deal of Egyptian cloth was intended for export in exchange for incense, myrrh, ebony, etc. This accounts for Alexandria's double role as a great textile center as well as a trading port.

Workshops and textile centers

We can not say where most of the Coptic fabrics we have were made, even when we know where they were dug up. Antinopolis, whose collection of fabrics needs to be studied with great care, itself presents great problems because of turn-of-the-century excavation methods.

The other cities renowned for their weavers' shops were Alexandria, Panopolis (Akhmin), Oxyrhynchus, and the Eastern side of the Delta (Tinnys and Damietta). Only two pieces of cloth bear the name of a place which could be where they were made: a piece at the Victoria and Albert Museum with the inscription Panos, which might mean Panopolis; 28 and a hanging in the Washington Textile Museum whose inscription can be read as Heracleus, which might mean Herakleopolis (although there is an Er-

The goddess Gaea
Tapestry. Linen and wool
5th century
25.5 x 23.9 cm
London, Victoria and Albert Museum; inv. 2137-1900
The goddess holds an ear of corn and cornucopia filled with flowers and fruits. The slight modeling effect of the draperies and cornucopia contrasts with the opacity of the silhouette and geometric design of the frame.

Tapestry with *putti**
Linen and wool
4th century
3.25 x 1.8 m
Washington D.C., The Textile
Museum; inv. 71.118
The alternation of numerous
geometric, floral and
figurative motifs contributes
to the overall effect and
shimmering splendor of the
complete piece. The *putti**,
holding birds, branches,
small dishes and wreaths,
are treated by color
gradation. The name
Herakleias, the town of
Heraclea is inscribed inside
one of these wreaths.

Tapestry "cartoon"
Papyrus
Turin, Egyptian Museum;
inv. suppl. 2200 bis.
Roughly sketched in ink, a
square is filled by small
black silhouettes placed
among animals and
vegetation. The fact that the
upper border decorated with
foliage scrolls was not
completed indicates its use
as a model. A right-angled
band with spearheads is still
visible along the left border.

egli near Constantinople as well as the town in Egypt).[29]

From the oldest pieces, with their strongly classicizing style and iconography (4th-5th centuries), it is obvious that the artisans had models in front of their eyes whose prototypes can be found in mosaics and paintings. Papyrus fragments with ink sketches of squares and braid decorated with foliage, flowers and figures have been compared to tapestry "artoons", and this seems right. There was one in the old Fouquet collection which was sold in 1922; another is conserved in the Turin Museum; and there are two more in the State Museum in Berlin.[30]

Beginning in the 6th century, there was a gradual Christianization of themes, and a clear break with classical forms. The use of cartoons is not so obvious: the fabrics give the impression that the artisans wove their tapestries without models, directly on the loom. This does not, of course, exclude a strong influence of fashion, something which is still true today in Egypt.

NOTES

1. Marie-Hélène RUTSCHOWSCAYA, 1986, p.53, n°143.
2. Marielle MARTINIANI-REBER, 1986.
3. Gabriel VIAL, 1985, p.50-51.
4. Ingrid BERGMAN, 1975, p.12-13.
5. Charles BACHATLY, 1961, p.47-49.
6. Dominique BENAZETH, 1989, p.219-228.
7. Marie-Hélène RUTSCHOWSCAYA, 1986, p.43-52.
8. R.J. FORBES, p.149-171.
9. Louisa BELLINGER, 1950, paper n°2.
10. Rodolphe PFISTER, 1934, p.81.
11. Ewa WIPSZYCKA, 1965, p.147.
12. Rodolphe PFISTER, 1935.
13. Marie-Hélène RUTSCHOWSCAYA, 1988, p.39-40.
14. François BARATTE, 1985, p.31-76.
15. Rodolphe PFISTER, 1935, p.14, n°57.
16. Edouard GERSPACH, 1987, p.130.
17. Albert GAYET, 1900, p.5-6.
18. H.E. WINLOCK et W.E. CRUM, 1926, p.9,68, n°2; 71-73; 155; 157.
19. Marie-Thérèse PICARD-SCHMITTER, 1965, p.296-321.
20. Marie-Hélène RUTSCHOWSCAYA, 1987, p.169-172.
21. Albert GAYET, 1900, p.5.
22. P. COLLINGWOOD, 1974.
23. Marie-Hélène RUTSCHOWSCAYA, Paris, 1987, p.478-481.
24. Charles DIEHL, 1933, p.503.
25. Ewa WIPSZYCKA, 1965, p.94.
26. H.E. WINLOCK et W.E. CRUM, 1926, p.9, 68, n°2; 71-73; 155; 157.
27. E. AMELINEAU, 1888, p.232.
28. A.F. KENDRICK, 1920, p.62, n°51, pl.XII.
29. James TRILLING, 1982, p.31, n°1, pl.1.
30. Collection du docteur Fouquet du Caire, 1922, n°109, pl.III.
- A.M. DONADONI-ROVERI, 1976, p.181-192.
- Arne EFFENBERGER, 1975, fig. 107.

Orbiculus* **with a cavalier**
Tapestry and tabby. Linen and wool
7-8th centuries
27 x 26.5 cm
Paris, Musée du Louvre, Department of Egyptian Antiquities; inv. AF 6255
The theme of horsemen, frequently found in Coptic iconography, is inherited from the great hunting scenes reproduced on the mosaics and sarcophagi of the Roman period.

41

FROM
TIME
TO SPACE

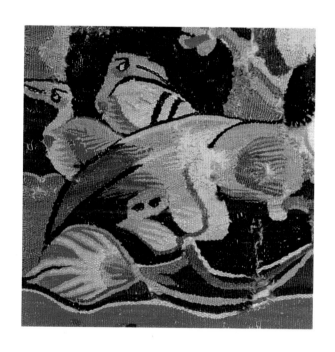

THE HISTORY OF DECORATED FABRICS

 An interest in decorated fabrics appears sporadically in the Pharaonic period. The almost exclusive use of linen, which is poorly suited to dyeing, generally produced white fabrics, sometimes brightened with several colored stripes.

This technical stringency appears to have suited the Egyptian taste, for these fabrics are also to be found in tombs of the Middle Kingdom next to foreigners dressed in multicolored robes.

No decorated fabrics dating from before the New Kingdom have survived. The oldest tapestries were found in the tomb of Thutmose IV[1] but the most significant collection was found in the tomb of Tutankhamen. This collection contained sumptuous tunics bearing woven and embroidered scenes with purely Egyptian motifs combined with iconography in the style of the Near East.[2] This fact, combined with growing relations with Oriental countries from the start of the New Kingdom, demonstrates an increasingly pronounced Egyptian taste for foreign fashion which became a veritable passion from the Greco-Roman period onwards. The Orientals were well versed in the custom of ornate fabrics. Numerous artifacts dating back to the period from the 14th to 12th centuries B.C. depict divine or royal figures wearing clothing decorated with varied geometric motifs.

Examples of fabrics representing the direct antecedents of Coptic fabrics were found in Palmyra and Dura Europos, Syria (2nd to 3rd centuries A.D.) From Dura Europos[3] come fabrics bearing red flowers with four petals on a green background; bands of waves, spots and fleurs de lys (Yale University); purplish red squares on a woven background of undyed linen (Louvre); a tunic with sleeves decorated with galloons. From Palmyra[4] comes a purple scarf with a geometric latticework worked on the flying shuttle; it is set off by an undyed linen bouclé background. The same site provided a fragment of a tunic with the neckline and the beginning of a galloon formed by a wide purple band embroidered with a row of stylized palmettes; the shoulder section is trimmed with a purple and ecru medallion with two interwoven squares forming a star enclosing a crown with eight circular motifs and a central rosette.

From the Roman period on, use of the tunic along with its decoration spread throughout the Mediterranean region: a praying figure (Rome, cemetery of Thrasea, middle of the 4th century), water carrier (Rome, Naples Museum, 4th century), candle bearer (Gargaresh, Libya, 4th century), slave (tomb of Silistra, Bulgaria, end of the 4th century).

The embroidered tunic discovered in the necropolis of Douch (Oasis of Khargeh) in 1984 demonstrates the appeal of rich ornamentation at the end of the 4th century.[5] This linen tunic is made of two sections of fabric joined together by seams at the shoulders and on the sleeves. The front and the back are decorated with a symmetrical scene. The plastron is formed by six friezes: two rows of interwoven hearts, a frontal view of a human head in the center of an interlace of rosettes, a row of palmettes, of row of bayonet-like lines and a row of pendants with alternating motifs. Falling from each shoulder, a band encloses a scroll of vines situated between two branches of ivy leaves; each ending in two ribbons from which hangs a naked winged figure holding in its hands a crown and a palm. On each shoulder there is a half medallion formed by a border with several friezes (waves, ivy branches, festoons and volutes). The center is occupied by a medallion formed by four serrated leaves enclosing a circle with a central dot bordered by two other points.

This custom persisted for a considerable length of time: the most famous example from the Byzantine period is the representation of a procession of the Empress Theodora on the mosaic of S. Vitale of Ravenna (6th century A.D.): The ladies of the court are wearing luxurious garments strewn with flowers, medallions, and squares with geometric patterns.

The Empress is draped in a wide cloak whose lower section shows the Magi bearing their gifts. From

Vegetal motif
Tapestry. Linen and wool
Dura Europus; 2nd-3rd
centuries

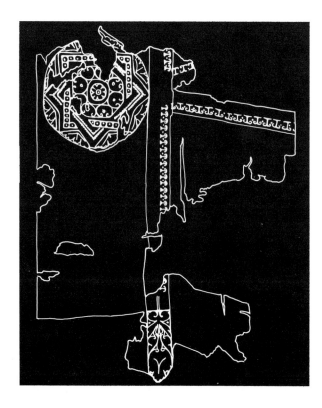

Fragment of a tunic
Linen and wool
Palmyra, Tomb of Elahbel
(built in 103 A.D.)
W. 1.25 m

the 4th century on, the Fathers of the Church and the members of the clergy objected to this artifice : "When they appear in public dressed in this manner, one could mistake them for painted murals...". "On these fabrics we see lions, panthers, bears, bulls, dogs, tree, cliffs, hunters, in short all that painters attempting to imitate nature can reproduce...". "The rich who have a vestige of piety select designs from the stories of the Gospel and have them reproduced by their workers. They believe that they please the Father by wearing these fabrics decorated with pious figures, but if they wish my advice they would do better to sell them and honor the living images of God." (Asterios Homelies, I "On the abuses of the rich").

THE PROBLEM OF CHRONOLOGY IN COPTIC FABRICS

Of the thousands of fragments unearthed in Egypt only two have been dated precisely. A medallion with geometric designs made of purple wool and linen from the tomb of Hawara (Fayum) was found with a coin dating back to approximately 340 A.D.[6] The tapestry, used as a shroud in the tomb of Aurelius Colluthius and his wife Tisoia in Antinoopolis, has been dated to the middle of the 5th century, on the basis of sales contracts and the papyrus testament both drawn up between 454 and 456 A.D. (Musée royaux d'Art et d'Histoire, Brussels).[7]

Excavations in the 19th century and at the beginning of the 20th century were not always carried out carefully or described in detail. Furthermore, movements of the earth, reduced space resulting in the piling of several bodies one on top of another and the

Medallions and band
Linen and wool
Hawara (Fayum), c. 340 A.D.

reusing of sepulchres falsified dating. For this reason, modern researchers also have to rely on technical analysis (fibres, dyes, weaving methods) and stylistic and iconographic studies based on comparison with other artistic fields in or outside Egypt (mosaics, reliefs, manuscripts, etc.).

Until now, all attempts at carbon-14 dating have failed to provide reliable results. In 1957-1958, an attempt by the Laboratory of the French Museums provided contradictory information on two samples taken from the same fragment.[8] American research at the Ohio State University and the University of Arizona in the eighties did not succeed in reducing the current margin of error of three hundred years; a margin incompatible with the Coptic period.

Initial research to establish the chronology of fabrics was undertaken by A.F. Kendrick in 1920 on the collection in the Victoria and Albert Museum in London.[9] He dated the end of Coptic art at the 13th century and determined three periods : a Greco-Roman period (3rd to 5th centuries), a transition period strongly marked by the Middle Eastern influence and the apparition of Christian symbols (5th and 6th centuries) and an entirely Christianized Coptic period (5th to 12th centuries). In 1924, M.S. Dimand,[10] followed by A. Wulff and W.F. Volbach in 1926,[11] confirmed these dates based on the decoration of the fabrics and comparison with mosaics. Technical studies by Rodolphe Pfister around 1935 completely innovated research methods by introducing scientific analysis.

For the first time, in 1938, Ernst Kühnel proposed the hypothesis of a "Coptic tradition in Muslim fabrics" dating back to the Fatimid period.[12] These fabrics are characterized by the use of wool and linen,

as was the Coptic custom, rather than silk. Tinnis, one of the most famous textile centers of the Arabic period, employed Coptic craftsmen. Private industry appears to have been the origin of similar production in Upper Egypt and in Fayum, where the Coptic tradition was well established. It was most probably the Tulunids who were responsible for the survival of this type of workshop whose tapestries show a definite predilection for highly stylized popular motifs. "We are therefore justified in speaking of a Coptic textile industry which was not only tolerated, but officially encouraged, in the second half of the 9th century parallel to the activity of workshops producing for export.[13]"

In two articles written in 1953,[14] Pierre du Bourguet referred to Ersnt Kühnel's conclusions and proposed an authoritative "working hypothesis" in his catalog of Coptic fabrics from the Louvre in 1964.[15] He based his hypothesis not only on the study of objects, but also on written accounts. A Persian traveller, Nasiri Khosrau, noted in the 11th century that weaving was the "exclusive right of the Copts"; at the end of the 10th century, the geographer Makkadasi stated that "a Copt cannot weave any fabric without the government's authorization," a statement which confirms the Persian's comment. Coptic fabrics were so famous that as far away as in India they were called *kabati* (plural of the Arab word *kobt* = Coptic), like muslins whose name was derived from Mosul.

The method consisted in regrouping the fabrics according to style and subject, on the basis of similar motifs recurring on different fragments. A second step aimed to date each group using a group of fabrics dated to the 12th century as a reference point. These fabrics had been clearly dated on the basis of parallels with art from the same period. The same principles were used for fabrics from the 6th century, making it possible to establish the stylistic characteristics and apply this method to fragments which were *a priori* from the chronological periods about which little was known. This was a major contribution as it represented a new vision of the chronology of the Coptic period up to the 12th century. It also led to the publication, in 1964, of an impressive catalog including approximately 1400 pieces presented in chronological groups. To this day, this catalog remains a valuable research tool.

USE OF THE FABRICS

Unfortunately, many fabrics have survived only as fragments, which makes it difficult to situate them in their original context. Nevertheless, the pieces which have survived in their original form

Aurelius Colluthius and his wife Tisoia
Tapestry. Linen and wool
Antinoopolis; mid-5th century
2.05 × 1.44 m
Brussels, Musées Royaux d'Art et d'Histoire; inv. Tx. 2470
This tapestry was discovered in a tomb and, according to a papyrus testament, can be dated to the middle of the 5th century. The treatment of heads and features permit the dating of other similar tapestries.

47

provide sufficient material for an almost complete picture of their use.

Clothing

The painted shrouds of the Roman mummies and the mosaics and paintings from the same period provide information on clothing in the 3rd and 4th centuries A.D.

On the shrouds, the deceased, surrounded by pharaonically inspired religious scenes, is portrayed in typically Roman style and technique. The men are most often dressed in white linen tunics, decorated with colored galloons on the chest and around the neckline. A shawl thrown over the shoulder is decorated with squares, medallions or swastikas*. The women's clothing is more elaborate and richer and, although it does include a white tunic, shows mainly colored tunics, decorated with galloons. The shawls are trimmed with a fringe and have wide bands surrounded by waves and enclosing foliage (Musée du Louvre)[16]. Others, draped around the figure, are decorated with large purple-violet medallions in which are raised geometric networks of interlacing, worked with the flying shuttle (Louvre[17], Vatican Museum)[18] identical to tapestries dated to the 4th century.

It was during this period that a radical transformation of antique dress began, first in the Orient and then in the rest of the Mediterranean. This transformation resulted from the invention of the woven, sewn tunic. In Egypt, along with draped clothing, a simple shape, known as the "sack tunic", dating back to the Middle Kingdom (around 2000-1780 B.C.),[19] was already familiar. This shape consisted of a folded and sewn linen rectangle; the upper section had an opening for the head and was often formed by several pieces of fabric, sewn together. This "sack tunic" could be folded and tightened around the waist by a wide pleated belt knotted in the front; the shape continued to be used up to the Roman era. A linen tunic with wide, but short sleeves found in Saqqara and dated to the 2nd century A.D. is entirely covered in scenes from Pharaonic mythology worked in red ink (Cairo Museum).[20] In the 4th century, the technique was innovated by weaving the tunic as a single section with a slit for the neckline. The garment was woven lengthwise on a loom. Weaving was started at one of the sleeves and worked through the body section and then completed with the other sleeve. This technique required a great width of warp. The sides were closed by sewn seams. The woven scenes, worked at

Tunic
Tapestry and tabby. Linen and wool
4th century
1.29 x 0.84 m
Moscow, The Pushkin Museum;
inv. 5823
The excellent state of preservation of this piece makes it a valuable example of the sumptuous decoration used on tunics during late antiquity. A very classical subject (with the use of the flying shuttle and alternation of undyed linen and colored wool yarns for the grounds) is successfully united with the unusually graceful silhouettes (dancers and Artemis between two heroes).

Lady Theodosia
Painting
Antinoopolis; 6th century
in situ
Flanked by Saint Colluthus and Saint Mary, Lady Theodosia is dressed in a tunic richly decorated with woven pieces containing geometric and animal motifs. She wears a mantle draped in the "antique" fashion and her hair, partly hidden by a light veil, is adorned with strings of pearls and cabochons in the Byzantine manner.

ΚΟΛΛΟΥΘΟC ΟΓΙΑ

the same time as the base fabric, were rarely sewn on. This type of garment is worn by figures on a burial painting from Antinoopolis showing the Lady Theodosia flanked by Saint Colluthus and Saint Mary (5th-6th centuries) ; she is dressed in a tunic with a richly decorated belt and a shawl. A veil, laden with strings of pearls, covers her hair. Worn by men, women and children alike, the tunic was either full length or stopped at the knee, it had narrow sleeves - long or short - and a belt to hold the folds of the garment in place. Woven, braided, knitted or tablet woven, the belts were both separate from the tunic or held in place by belt loops. Two bouclé tapestries (Louvre,[21] Museum of Fine Arts, Boston[22]) both show a figure wearing this type of tunic under an aedicule with a pediment.

The elements of the scene were formed by galloons *(clavi)*, medallions *(orbiculi)* and squares *(tabulae)*. The number and arrangement of these forms varies from one piece to another and appears to be a chronological indication, with a tendency to excess starting in the Arabic period. Narrow or wide *clavi* were the only decoration on the front and back of these garments ; sometimes galloons were also used on the sleeves. These *clavi* started at the shoulder and stopped at the knee or the chest. When they ended at the chest, they often did so in the shape of a spearhead or a leaf. On the shoulders and the lower sec-

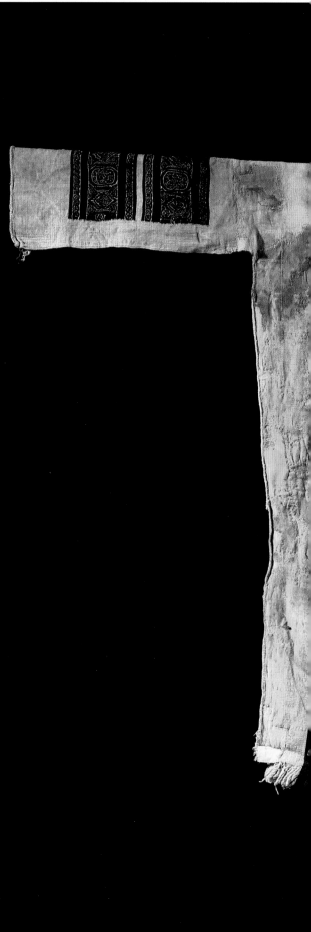

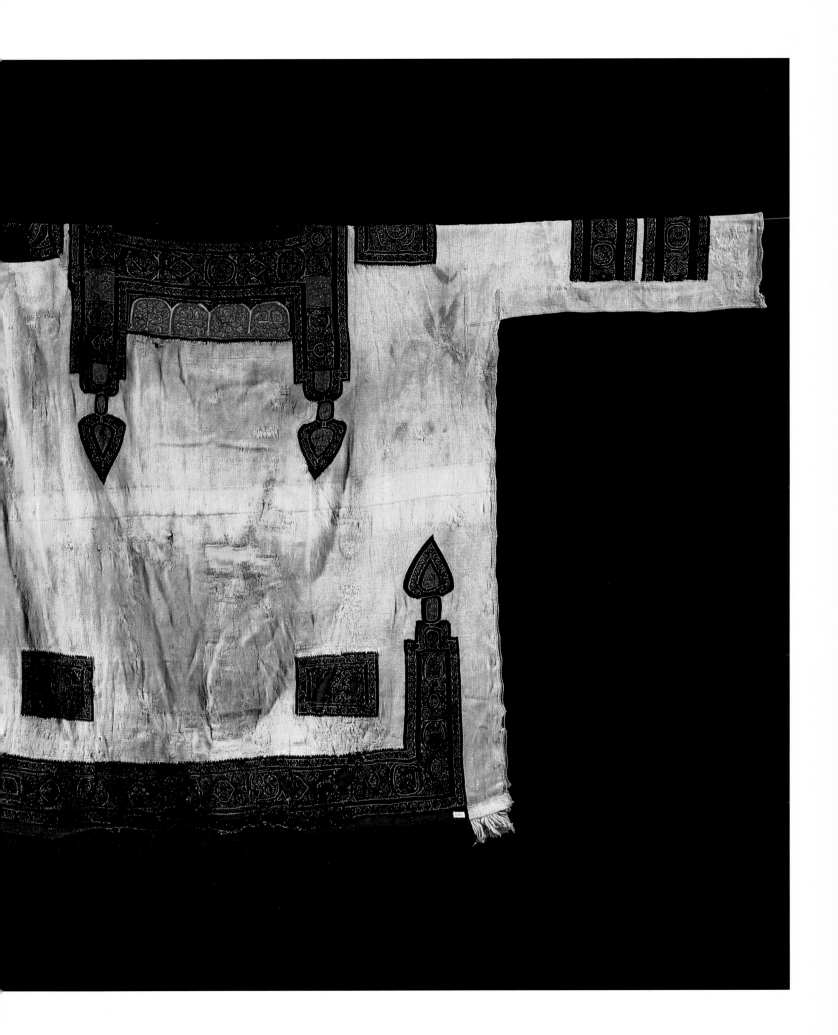

tion of the tunic were the *tabulae* or the *orbiculi* encircled by square-edged galloons. The neckline was sometimes undecorated, but it could be surrounded by galloons, which could even form rectangular plastrons or extend to the neckline and be richly decorated.

The tunic from the Pushkin Museum (4th century) is a fine example of this type of garment[23] : the plastron is formed by two rows of superimposed arcatures. Those in the top row contain six warriors and those in the bottom row show Artemis between two heroes and two groups of two dancers ; the *clavi* on the sleeves and the body are formed by a stylized scroll of alternating vine leaves, animals and warriors.

The tunics were often worn over each other. The thinnest tunics were worn like "undershirts", under the thicker ones, although they are not fundamentally different and their decoration is often identical.

For a long period they were incorrectly referred to as dalmatics.[24] In fact, dalmatic refers to a specific garment, of which only two examples were found in Egypt : one is displayed in the Victoria and Albert Museum[25] and the other in the Musée du Louvre. They are both long white garments reaching down to the ground, decorated with purple bands extending down to the lower section and with galloons on the sleeves. They are characterized by the absence of a belt and by the length and width of the sleeves (Veneranda and Saint Petronila, cemetery of Domitilia, Rome, 4th century). They are said to have been borrowed from the Dalmatians by the Romans in the 2nd century A.D. and were, at this time, considered an effeminate garment. It was not until the 4th century that they were definitively adopted and became the insignia of the deacons.

Children's garments, widening towards the bottom, began to appear from the 4th century on. The sleeves, extending only slightly, were trimmed with a brocaded galloon. The sleeves and shoulders were decorated with strewn, brocaded or embroidered scenes. Embroidered sections were often sewn on ; a technique which was rare in the earlier period. The excessive decoration was commonly emphasized by the use of colored wools and trims, laden with decorative galloons and pads or increasingly thick fringes. During the Arab period (10th century), the custom of producing these tunics entirely from woolen tapestries spread ; silk ornaments were frequently sewn on to the tapestries. It was not until the end of the 12th century that a new type of tunic, similar to the modern jallabeh*, became popular : this tunic was sewn together from several sections of linen canvas and had long, narrow sleeves and a vertical slit at the chest ; silk was used for the striped patterns, or on the more elaborate garments, for the embroidered scenes.[26]

The garment normally referred to as a "mantle", made of woollen tapestry, is often simply a rectangular section with a slit allowing it to be pulled over the head. Some of these garments have a hood and short, slit sleeves or long sleeves. The Louvre possesses a small child's coat with a hood, bearing scenes similar to those found on tunics.[27] The main difference between the two types of garment is the weight of the fabric : mantles are made of heavier fabric.

Tapered mantles, of a widening shape, with very long sleeves and cuffs trimmed with galloons, were found in Antinoopolis. They were made of wool felt or floss silk and decorated with stiched-on silk galloons (Staatliche Museen, Berlin,[28] Musée Historique des Tissus).[29] They must be ceremonial mantles of Sassanid* origin, as they were found with leggings and tunics with a slit collar trimmed with silk borders (Staatliche Museen).

A shawl is a rectangular piece of fabric which was worn by men, women and children. The edges were often trimmed with fringes, sometimes placed after open-work sections. The backgrounds were either of linen canvas or linen bouclé and the scenes raised in wool and linen tapestry. The praying figure at a stele, standing between two crosses below an aedicule, from the Cairo Museum[30] wears a shawl around its neck and arms. Each fold is decorated with a square containing a rosette and trimmed with a fringe. The large shawls (up to two meters) have symmetrical designs of squares, medallions, leaves, stars and swastikas* in the four corners and may have an identical motif in the center. The corner patterns are often surrounded by square-edged galloons (Sabine shawl 6th century, Louvre).[31]

The "Shawl of vines" (Louvre)[32] has a sumptuous border of two large bands containing vine scrolls and bright red flowers. This shawl is similar to the one worn by the "Woman with *crux ansata*", found on the canvas from a 4th century mummy (Louvre)[33] : around her shoulders she wears a luxurious shawl with bands of scrolls enclosed by lines of waves.

Smaller shawls are decorated with simple galloons of leaves or stylized scrolls.

Shawls appear to have gone out of fashion during the Arab period. This hypothesis is confirmed by the absence of large shawls. The linen canvas backgrounds then gave way to tapestries of colored wool and the edges were finished with thick fringes or simple woven borders.

Leggings, worn by horsemen or hunters, appeared in the Byzantine period. This garment was adopted from Parthia by the Sassanids* and the Palmyrians

who transmitted it to Egypt where it was adapted to local taste. The Palmyrian Museum contains sculptures (1st to 3rd centuries A.D.) of male figures wearing this type of leg covering. On paintings from Bawit (8th century), Saint Sisinnios is shown on horseback, wearing leggings, as are the gazelle hunters.[34] A long flared tube of woolen material, silk or leather is secured by a belt hidden under the tunic: "A coarse leather belt with suspenders holds up the leggings at the sides.[35]" They are decorated with a single galloon along the edges (Louvre)[36] or the entire legging is covered with orientally inspired geometric designs (Musée Historique des Tissus;[37] Louvre[38]). Albert Gayet discovered numerous examples of leggings in tombs in Antinoopolis which apparently date back to the Byzantine period (5th and 6th centuries): "Leggings of grey-yellow rep, trimmed with a large tapestry band on the lower section, forming a litre with four stripes and flowering scrolls. The band contains a set of medallions with human heads, raised on yellow backgrounds positioned in green squares."[39]

Mosaics and sculptures from the Greco-Roman period show workers, playing girls (mosaics from Piazza Armerina, 4th century, Sicily) or martyrs dressed in a simple garment tied around the waist *(perizoma)*. However, the only undergarments which have been found are pants or long underpants of cotton and silk, indicating a later date. They are sewn together from several tapered sections (Louvre[40], Musées Royaux d'Art et d'Histoire, Brussels).[41]

The custom of covering the head was typically

Coat with hood
Tapestry. Wool
11th century
63 x 82 cm
Paris, Musée du Louvre, Department of Egyptian Antiquities; inv. E 26525
This child's coat is fitted with a hood sewn to the neckline. The style of the animals decorating the inset-bands suggest a late date.

Shawl of vines
Tapestry and tabby.
Linen and wool
5th century
134 x 80.5 cm
Paris, Musée du Louvre,
Department of Egyptian
Antiquities; inv. AF 6113
The magnificent colors
employed for the decoration
of this shawl evoke the
equally splendid moasaics at
Ravenna (5-6th centuries).
The same vine foliage scrolls
and red flowers covered the
palace walls and constituted
the ornamental decoration
of palace curtains as well as
clothing of religious figures
and ladies of the court.

Fragment of a legging
Tapestry. Wool
Antinoopolis; 5-6th centuries
Lyon, Musée Historique des
Tissus; inv. 28928
This piece of clothing and its
decoration are typically
Sassanian*. The enthroned
king, the mounted archers
and the network of
geometric motifs were
probably copied from
Sassanian silk fabrics or
silver vases.

feminine. Simple veils, or the edges of scarfs and shawls were used for this purpose. However, there were also special coifs in the form of nets, headrolls or bonnets.

The linen or wool nets were made using the Sprang technique, which was for some time thought to be like lace (Louvre).[42] The rectangular section was rolled and then knotted to form a cone.

Rolls, made either of multicolored wool or fabric stuffed with wool, were positioned on these nets (Louvre, Berlin Museum). Some of them were covered with an open-work or golden leather band (Louvre).[43] The stucco statuette (Louvre)[44] shows a seated young girl wearing a tunic decorated on the shoulders and legs with clavi* and heart-shaped motifs. Her hair is crowned by a pink and black striped roll, identical to the hairstyles from Antinoopolis, where this figurine was found.

Wool bonnets, most likely for children, formed by several sections, lined and sewn together, were designed to cover the head and the ears. A cord under the chin was used to hold them in place. The only decoration was crosses which were either woven or formed by two crossed ribbons (Louvre : Arab period?)

Woven or knitted wool socks sometimes had a cross in the upper section (child's sock found by Albert Gayet in Antinoopolis, 8th century?). Socks with a separate big toe were designed to be worn with sandals (Victoria and Albert Museum),[45] but most socks were "ankle socks" tied at the ankle with a cord.

It is difficult to determine whether the so-called "sacks", made by the same Sprang technique as the head nets, were in fact used as sacks or coifs. A painting from Wadi Sarga (Middle Egypt), (Victoria and Albert Museum)[46] and two stelaes (Cairo Museum[47]; Staatcliche Museen, Berlin)[48] show figures carrying sacks bearing Egyptian crosses, either in their hands or over their arms. Their triangular (V) or square shape and their decoration resemble those of objects housed in the Louvre and the Victoria and Albert Museum[49]. Other "sacks" with loose stitches could not have been used as sacks despite their shape and the presence of fine cords (Louvre)[50].

Discrimination against the Christians, starting from the 8th century, required that they wear distinctive garments : a black robe secured by a black belt (zunnar), a yellow turban and a piece of fabric (qhiyar) bearing a cross distinguished them from the Muslim population. Nevertheless, the shape of the Coptic garments survived to the 12th century. At this time clothing changed dramatically, leading to the disappearance of the Coptic tunic, which had been a Egyptian symbol for over nine centuries.

The pieces described thus far were all secular clothing. Religious garments were distinct in that they were worn by those who had decided to leave the world and retreat to the desert.[51]

For this reason, hermits and anchorites* dressed in rags or even shrouds, clearly indicating that they had abandoned worldly concerns.

Vague archeological and literary sources, render the study of religious costumes arduous. Tombs in monasteries contained both laymen and monks and it is often difficult to distinguish between them. The pieces most often discovered are linen shrouds secured around the body by narrow linen bands in a "lattice" pattern, recalling the ancient Pharaonic methods.

The same problem occurs in the study of iconographic documents as they often portray monks in lay clothing or Saints in sumptuous ceremonial clothing.

This is why at the beginning of Christianity in Egypt there were no rules governing the attire of clerics and monks. Choice of clothing was a matter of individual responsibility. The first occurrences of symbolism in religious clothing, based on the teachings of Saint Anthony and Saint Pachomius, are found in the 4th and 5th centuries. Even so, the fragments which have been uncovered are too incomplete to substantiate classification of religious garments, in the manner of secular clothing.

Furnishing fabrics

Some of the numerous pieces of fabric housed in museums and belonging to church collections were complete or partial garments, others were obviously used for furnishing, even if their decoration is often the same as that of items of clothing.

Their exact usage is much more difficult to determine as they are generally square or rectangular panels without any distinguishing features.

However, on the basis of monuments and texts, it is possible to determine the use of the large fabrics, many of which were discovered in necropoles where they were reused as shrouds.

A mosaic from Ravenna shows the main entrance to the palace of the Emperor Theodoric (S. Apollinare Nuovo, 6th century): the central door is blocked by a curtain decorated with galloons at right angles, showing geometric patterns, similar to those found on some of the shawls. A similar tapestry covered with a multitude of grape-gathering putti* is housed in the Louvre.[52] Curtains covered with a scattering of flowers close off the side entrances.

The custom of concealing the entrances to buildings was not limited to secular buildings ; church en-

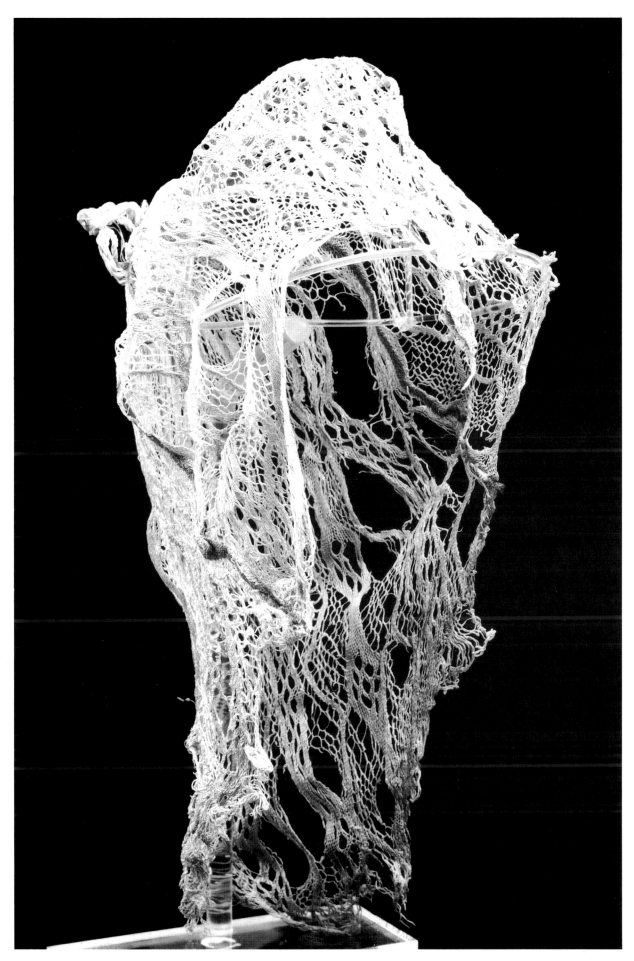

Head net
Sprang*. Linen
Coptic period
L. 24 cm
Paris, Musée du Louvre,
Department of Egyptian
Antiquities; AF 5868
The sprang technique was
used for head nets and for
the so-called "sacks" (?).

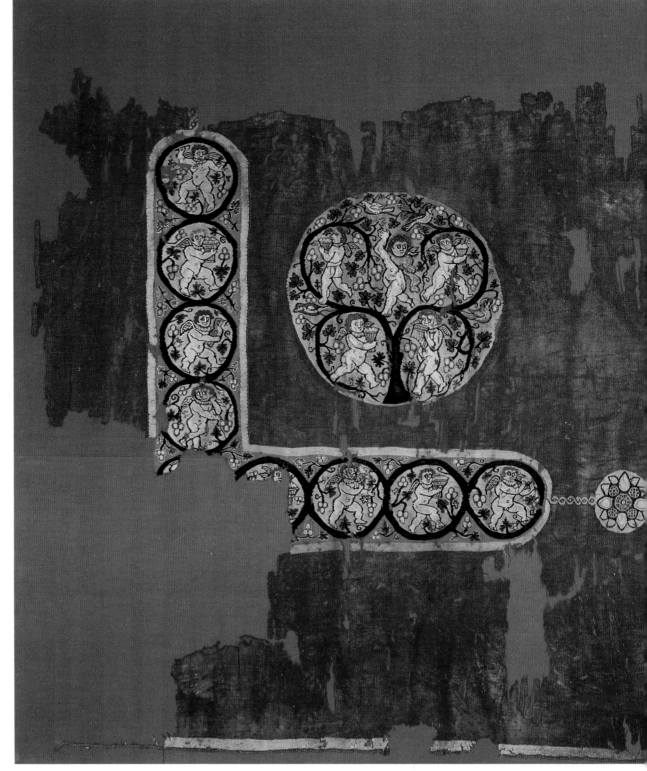

Textile with *putti* gathering grapes
Tapestry. Linen and wool
6th century
162 x 97.5 cm
Paris, Musée du Louvre,
Department of Egyptian
Antiquities; inv. E 27205
The same composition, in
reverse, would have
appeared in the missing
part of the tapestry. The
same layout can be seen in
shawls, altar cloths and
curtains. The piece's bacchic
characteristic is
demonstrated by the
presence of grapepicking
*putti**, dancers, musicians
and by the wine-colored
ground treated entirely in
tapestry weave, evoking the
lees at the bottom a barrels.

Detail : The theme of vine
shoots (*orbiculi**) whose
coils shelter the *putti*, is
repeated on sarcophagi
reliefs and mosaics of the
Roman period. P. 62

trances were covered by the same type of curtain as is demonstrated by a mosaic showing a basilica with its entrances concealed by knotted curtains (Louvre, 5th century).[53] Even inside, the columns had curtains which could be used to separate the naves or block the view to the sanctuary (Saint Mennes praying between two camels in front of the chancel of his pilgimage basilica, ivory carving, 6-7th centuries, Milan, Castello Sforzesco).

A description of Hagia Sophia of Constantinople (Descriptio S. Sophiae, II, vs. 340), mentions tapestries which hung from the columns of the *ciborium** of the altar; it states that "this decoration was not worked by laborious passing of a needle through fabric, but on a shuttle using various colours and different weights of thread provided by the silkworm."

The same types of fabrics were also used as altar cloths : in a scene depicting the sacrifices of Abel and

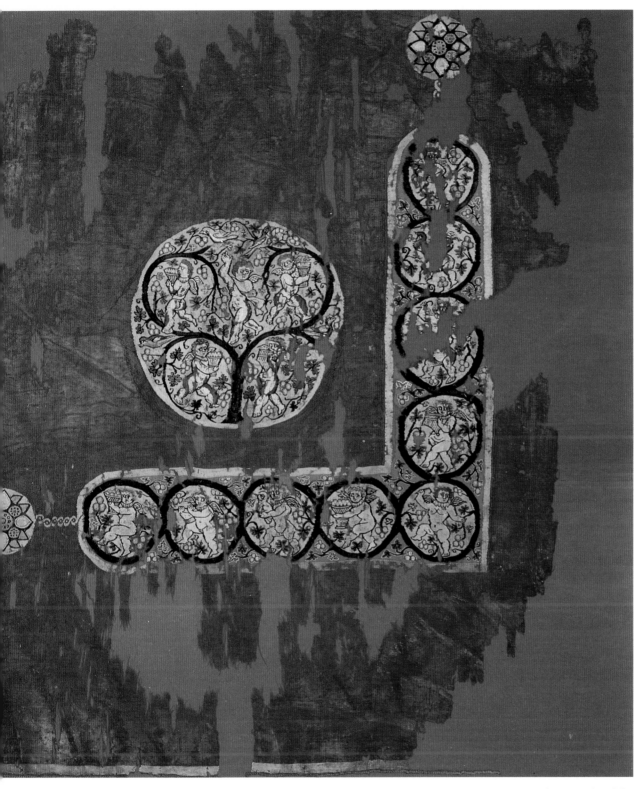

Melchizedech on a mosaic from S. Vitale in Ravenna (6th century), the altar is shown covered by two superimposed cloths decorated with the same star pattern and galloons at right angles. The upper cloth, like the shawls, is bordered by fringes.

On the *Ashburnam Pentateuch** (Paris, Bibliotèque Nationale, 7th century), the granting of the Tablets of the Law to Moses on Mount Sinai shows the tabernacle as a basilica sanctuary: the chancel,

the columns and the altar are draped in similar fabrics.

The altar of Hagia Sophia of Constantinople was covered by a cloth depicting Christ between two of his Disciples, Peter and Paul; the borders show the miracles of Christ and the good deeds of Justinian and Theodora.

The veils with printed Biblical scenes in the Berlin Museum (Granting of the Tablets of Law) and the

61

Victoria and Albert Museum (Moses receiving the Commandments, the resurrection of Lazarus, the Annunciation, the Nativity scene, Saint Thomas, Saint Peter and Saint Paul) may also have been used as altar cloths or curtains.

It is highly likely that walls which were not covered with mosaics were hung with storied tapestries intended to be admired by the visitors demonstrating the beliefs of the owner or the sacred character of the site.

The most famous piece, dating back to Late Roman Antiquity (4th century A.C.) is a fabric printed by resist dyes on linen know as the "veil of Antinoopolis" (Louvre). With its three types of decoration –a grand Dyonisian procession, a scroll with birds in the middle and a series of scenes depicting Dionysus' childhood– this hanging must have adorned the private residence of a rich inhabitant of Antinoopolis whose pagan faith was still strong.

Another fine example is provided by the fragments of a linen and wool tapestry, shared between three museums (4th-5th centuries). Satyr and Maenad (Cleveland Museum), Dionysus leaning against a column (Boston Museum), cithara player (Abegg Stiftung, Bern).

Tapestries worked in linen and wool provided a large background bursting with the sumptuous colors of extremely varied iconographies recalling the scenes of mosaics and painting : Two Nereids ; a boar hunt (Dumbarton Oaks); Nereids and dolphins ; geometric lattices and putti* ; aedicule with pediment (The Textile Museum); *crux ansata* and Jonas leaving the mouth of the whale (Louvre); the ascension of Elijah (Abegg Stiftung)[54].

In Antinoopolis, the heads of some of the deceased rested on a cushion with a cover. Fragments of these covers indicate that they were worked on the draw loom. The tapestry weave is entirely covered with, repeating geometric patterns, the colors being reversed on the back so that there was no "wrong side" to the work. The use of this type of cover[55] is illustrated by a painting from Saqqara depicting Christ, on a throne, seated on a cushion decorated with a lattice pattern and trimmed with a row of pearls (6th century).

THE STYLISTIC EVOLUTION OF COPTIC FABRICS

Once the background for a chronological study and the methods of technical analysis have been established, we can proceed, on the basis of several examples, to study the changes in the style of Coptic fabrics.

It is highly probable that the busts of the Nile god

(Pushkin Museum) and the Goddess Gaea (Hermitage) dated back to the end of the 2nd or 3rd century. Comparisons with mosaic floors from Antinoopolis substantiate this dating : in the House of the Calendar, a depiction of Oceanus (2nd century) worked in high relief, shows that the weaver of the Nile god and Gaea practically transposed a mosaic or painting into his technique.[56] The background of the mosaic is entirely covered by an ocean scene with a multitude of fish. The strong relief and the shading used to produce three dimensions are found on two fragments of tapestry with the same composition (Louvre and Musée Historique des Tissus). A scroll of fruits, pecked at by birds (Victoria and Albert Museum) appears to be taken directly from the decorated tunic of an inhabitant of Palmyra in the middle of 2nd century (Louvre).[57] The large series of ornaments on linen cloth, squares or purple-violet medallions woven of geometric latticework are treated on the "flying shuttle" with a precision which was never to be equalled.

This period is marked by a strong naturalist tendency which lasted through to the following centuries (4th-5th centuries), but with rounder, heavier shapes. The tapestry of the *putti* in a boat (British Museum) is a fine example of this naturalism. However, the silhouettes and the faces show a tendency towards stylization of the features : the eyes are enlarged and marked by a heavy circle (woman's head, Detroit ; dancer's head, Louvre). Relief, created by color gradation, was still widely used. Large hangings with Dionysian subjects have these characteristics, sometimes accompanied by a deformation of the body : the Maenad and Satyr from the Cleveland Museum have feet with fan-like toes : the Maenad's wide hips are out of proportion with the rest of her body and her breasts are placed too high and too close together.

Around the tapestry portraying Aurelius Colluthus and his wife, Tisoia, dated to the middle of the 5th century, we can group pieces of similar style such as Atalanta and Meleager (British Museum), a galloon with figures (Abegg Stiftung), two Nereids (Dumbarton Oaks).

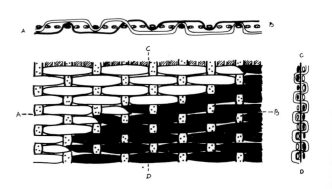

Lion and boar hunt
Tapestry. Wool
5-6th centuries
94 x 81.7 cm
Washington D.C., Dumbarton Oaks
Collection; inv. 37.14
Dressed in pants or leggings
and short oriental-style
tunics, the two hunters are
equipped with bows in
imitation of Sassanian*
hunting scenes. Curiously,
the frame of the border
contains a marine decor of
fish, shrimp and shellfish of
which similar fragments are
found in the Abbeg Stiftung
and the Musée de Cluny.

Architectural motif
Tapestry and tabby. Linen and
wool
4th century
2.13 x 1.17 m
Washington D.C., The Textile
Museum; inv. 71.18
A curtain decorated with
clusters of grapes and birds
appears to be hung between
the columns. The columns
with capitals of stylzied
acanthus motifs, support a
pediment with perched
birds. This is an
arrangement frequently
used by stelae sculptors who
often replace the birds with
wild beasts or fish. The
pediment is sculpted in a
square motif with a pearl
border enclosing four red
blossoming flowers; a theme
frequently represented on
Coptic fabrics and Byzantine
mosaics.

Orbiculus* with goddess Gaea
Tapestry. Linen and wool
3-4th centuries
D. 25.5 cm
Leningrad, Hermitage Museum;
inv. 11440
Attesting to religious
syncretism, the Greek
goddess Gaea, identified by
an inscription near her face,
assumes the attributes of
the goddes Isis; a winged
solar disk, earrings in the
form of uraei* and the knot
of Isis. The pendant of the
Nile god at the Pushkin
Museum, Gaea is executed
in a more schematic style
which places this tapestry a
little later.

During the following period (6th-7th centuries),
the illusion effect tends to be eliminated and replaced by flat tints and increasing use of the "flying
shuttle", making it possible to compensate for the
lack of relief by outlining the interior details of an
object. The 7th century appears to have been a turning point during which use of the relief method died
out. The tapestry of Dionysus with an Isis-like figure
(Louvre) or the Nereid holding a goblet (Cleveland
Museum) have bodies formed by hatched contours,
whose effect is a definite departure from the softness
of the relief effect of the earlier period. The *Orbiculus* of the Nile god (Louvre) depicts a scene from
Greco-Roman mythology (personification of the river, sea goddess, *putti** worked with Greek style
forms, but already tending towards an entirely Coptic style: flat tints and use of the "flying shuttle"
combined with a tendency towards dislocation of the
body and the large, stylized, fixed eyes, found in the
following period. The vegetal motifs also tend to be

simplified and the whorls of the scrolls are separated
in series of medallions combined with two stylized
birds (7th 8th centuries). Fabrics with scrolls drawn
in clear linear style can be compared to the stays of
the Dome of the Rock (691), characterized by the fil-
iform style of the foliage.

For the Islamic period (7th-8th centuries), comparison of fabrics with contemporary art led Pierre
du Bourguet to distinguish a group of tapestries
with a purple-violet background worked with the
flying shuttle, but differing in style from the group
dated to the 4th century. The geometric figures are
filled with a trellised network, rosettes with eight
lobes and hexagons whose thickness gives them the
appearance of embroidery. The "enchenillage" effect
on some of the models can be compared to the leather bindings from Kairouan with their stamped
scenes (9th-13th centuries).[58] The progressive departure from realistic forms accompanied by an increasing *horror vacui* and the intricacy of geometric

patterns reflect the tendencies of Islamic art where pure decoration plays an important role : the ornamental composition of woodwork (doors, mushrabeyeh*), sculptures (Mosque in Ibn Toulonn, 9th century), the frames of cruciform leaves surrounding miniatures, the "Sassanid rooster"* motif, typical of Fatimid silks, the alternating of spread flowers and half-flowers (Dome of the Rock, Jerusalem, 8th century) are all patterns which belong to this later period. A fragment of a woolen tapestry (Cairo, Museum of Islamic Art) bears a Kufic* inscription naming the site of production (Kais, Upper Egypt) and the date (784-785 A.D.) : clearly identifiable fish swim among stylized palmettes and are surrounded by friezes of hearts, losanges and a trefoil border.[59]

Kufic inscriptions are also to be found on tapestries with highly stylized human figures (8th-10th centuries) which evolved until the 12th century towards forms which dissolve in a colored mosaic.

"The style is of varying degrees of purity, but it shows great liberty of compostion and workmanship ; it is devoid of minute detail and subtleties, even when we have difficulty understanding the artist's intentions. When it is not related to Roman decoration or Oriental art, it is orignal ; it has a unique character, a particular flavor, whether it is fine like our lace or thick and dull like the ornaments of inferior races ; it represents, as a popular, intimate display, a special type which will soon be referred to as the Coptic sytle" (Ernest Gerspach).

Orbiculus of the Nile god
Tapestry. Linen and wool
3rd century
29.6 x 29.4 cm
Moscow, Pushkin Museum ; inv. 5822
The pendant of the goddess Gaea at the Hermitage, the execution of this tapestry makes use of a more subtle and "pictorial" color gradation. As with all river personifications of the Roman period, the Nile is shown as an old man in heroic semi-nudity, holding a conucopia. The pink lotus above his head is the incarnate symbol of Nilotic* vegetation.

Fragment with a fish
Tapestry. Wool
Antinoopolis, 3rd century
1.38 x 0.87 m
Lyon, Musée Historique des
Tissus; inv. 28927
An identical, but smaller
(49 x 35.5 cm), fragment is
conserved in the Musée du
Louvre. The aquatic subject
as well as the treatment of
the shadows and modeling
of the the fish by color
gradation show the weaver's
familiarity with mosaics and
paintings.

Amorini in a boat
Weft looped wool on linen warp
Akmin; 6th century
London, British Museum; inv. 20717

This might be the reproduction of a detail of a marine mosaic illustrating a triumph of Neptune (Musée du Louvre; inv. Ma. 1880)

Galloons with figures
Tapestry. Linen and wool
5th century
1.47 x 0.58 m
Bern (Riggisberg) Abegg Stiftung; inv. 1385

Similar galloons are found in the Abegg Stiftung (inv. 1025) and in the Staatliche Museum Preussiches Kulturbesitz, Berlin. Their composition resembles the galloons bordering the piece of textile representing a flutist (Coptic Musuem, Cairo). They too must have been included in the decoration with a linen ground.

Head of a dancer
Tapestry. Wool
4-5th centuries
42 x 32 cm
Paris, Musée du Louvre,
Department of Egyptian
Antiquities ; inv. AF 6148

The style and inconography
of this fragment indicate
that it should be placed
within the same context as
the figures in the Dionysian
tapestry conserved in the
Abegg Stiftung in
Riggisberg.

Nereid holding a bowl
Tapestry. Linen and wool
7th century
67.7 x 64.8 cm
Cleveland, Museum of Art;
inv. 53.18

The clumsy manner of representing the torso, breasts and highlighting of the drapery excludes this work from the mainstream of classical tradition in antiquity. The stylized border with a bird in the middle is treated in flat colors placing this piece in a period when classical conventions had already been forgotten.

71

Square with a nereid
Tapestry. Linen and wool
7th century
23.5 x 23.2 cm
Paris, Musée du Louvre,
Department of Egyptian
Antiquities; inv. AF 5467
The decor of the border
consists of a foliage scroll
that has attained the
ultimate stage of evolution.
Each whorl has become a
red disk marked with a
black "S". The nereid
straddles a sea monster and
lifts a veil with one hand
forming an arch over her
head.

Fragment of a coat
Tapestry. Linen and wool
12th century
30 x 28 cm
Paris, Musée du Louvre,
Department of Egyptian
Antiquities; inv. E 26735
This fragment is the bottom
part of a coat trimmed in a
thick fringe. The end of the
Coptic period is
characterized by the use of
the flying shuttle in
enchenillage to treat
rosettes with eight sepals,
motifs current on objects of
Muslim art. The four
dancers are conceived as
mere token figures.

NOTES

1. E. RIEFSTAHL, 1944.
2. G.M. CROWFOOT and N. de GARIES DAVIES, 1941, p. 113-138.
3. Rodolphe PFISTER et Louisa BELLINGER, 1945.
4. Rodolphe PFISTER, I, 1934; II, 1937; III, 1940.
5. Françoise DUNAND and Roger LICHTENBERG, 1985, p. 133-148, pl. XXII-XXVII.
6. W.M. FLINDERS PETRIE, 1889, pl. XXI.
7. Jacqueline LAFONTAINE-DOSOGNE, 1988, fig. 17.
8. Pierre du BOURGUET, 1957, p. 1-31. Pierre du BOURGUET, 1958, p. 52-63.
9. A.F. KENDRICK, 1920.
10. Maurice S. DIMAND, 1924.
11. A. WULFF and W.F. VOLBACH, 1926.
12. Ernst KÜHNEL, 1938, p. 79-89.
13. Ernst KÜHNEL, 1938, p. 85-86.
14. Pierre du BOURGUET, 1953, p. 1-31. Pierre du BOURGUET, III, 1953, p. 167-174.
15. Pierre du BOURGUET, 1964.
16. Inv. Nos. AF 6440 and 6487.
17. Inv. No. AF 6485.
18. Inv. No. 17953.
19. Jean-Luc BOVOT, 1986, p. 74-80.
20. Paul PERDRIZET, 1934, XXXIV, p. 97-128.
21. Inv. No. E 10530.
22. Inv. No. 49315.
23. R. SHURINOVA, 1967, No. 5.
24. Dominique BOUCHET, 1981.
25. A.F. KENDRICK, 1920, p. 40, No. 1, pl. I.
26. Dominique PFISTER, 1981.
27. Inv. No. E 26525.
28. Inv. No. E 14231.
29. Marielle MARTINIANI-REBER, 1986, p. 54, No. 22.
30. Inv. No. 8687.
31. Inv. No. E 29302.
32. Inv. No. AF 6113.
33. Inv. No. AF 6487.
34. Jean CLEDAT, 1904, fasc. 2, pl. LV-LVI; 1916, pl. XVI-XVII.
35. Albert GAYET, 1898, p. 9.
36. Inv. No. MG 1234.
37. Inv. No. 233.
38. Inv. No. MG 39.
39. Albert GAYET, 1898, p. 28-29.
40. Inv. No. AF 6093.
41. Inv. No. 425.
42. Inv. Nos. AF 5866, 5867, 5868.
43. Inv. No. E 13948.
44. Inv. No. E 12429. *Un siècle de fouilles françaises en Egypte*, 1981, No. 359. p. 344.
45. A.F. KENDRICK, 1921, Nos. 592 and 593.
46. Inv. No. G 1.14.
47. Inv. No. 8705.
48. Inv. No. 9624.
49. Pierre du BOURGUET, 1964, F 247 F 249. A.F. KENDRICK, 1921, Nos. 600, 602, 605.
50. Inv. No. AF 5872.
51. Nicole Morfin, 1983.
52. Inv. No. E 27205.
53. Inv. No. MA 3676 (département des A.G.E.R.).
54. Marie-Hélène RUTSCHOWSCAYA, Guiry-en-Vexin, 1986, p. 142-143.
55. Coptic Museum, Cairo, Inv. No. 7989. J.E. QUIBELL, 1909, pl. VIII.
56. Doro LEVI, 1947, pl. VI.
57. Inv. No. AO 2398 (département des antiquités orientales).
58. Pierre du BOURGUET, 1953, p. 16-18.
59. John BECKWITH, 1959, p. 24.

Orbiculus with Christ between two imperial figures (?)
Tapestry. Linen and wool. 10th century. 20.5 x 1.83 cm
Paris, Musée du Louvre, Department of Egyptian Antiquities; inv. AF 5737
The positioning of the three figures on this piece
is based on Byzantine ex voto in mosaics or stone
representing Christ or the Virgin accompanied by an imperial couple.

THE IMAGE, MIRROR OF A CIVILIZATION

On the whole, Coptic art inherited very few characteristics from Pharaonic art. By the time Coptic art came into existence, Egypt had already been invaded by Greek and then, Roman forms, whose fusion with Pharaonic themes produced results that were either curious or successful.[1]

The same tendency continued in the following centuries. The representation of subjects taken from the Pharaonic repertory and adapted to the style of the period was not uncommon. The so-called "Nilotic"* subjects by the popular Alexandrian artist, Demetrius Topographos, Ptolemy VI's painter, were extremely fashionable in the Roman world. The gallon and border of the *orbiculus** of "Sabine shawl" (Louvre) are covered with *putti** astride crocodiles, fishing in boats or catching birds; the latter posture could be a derivative of the celebrated swimmers of the Pharaonic period. The iconographical antecedents of the "Nilotic"* representations are illustrated by the famous scenes of hunting and fishing so frequently reproduced on the carved or painted walls of the tombs from the Ancient Empire (the tombs of Menna and Nakht, 18th dynasty). These themes, also used in Roman mosaics and paintings, were to become "clichés" that were used as models for all mediums. Thus, the presence of the pink lotus, formed by a rigid corolla scattered with seeds, indicates the spread of Nilotic* landscapes by means of cartoons. Imported from India in the Ptolemaic period, it has constantly been represented in this type of scene (the Palestrina mosaics, Italy, 1st century A.D.). Nevertheless, contrary to the Roman custom of materializing aquatic elements (waves or peninsulas) in the form of emerging visible parts only, the Coptic artisans set their scenes against a neutral background where nothing was concealed. The convention appeared in Egypt very long ago and became characteristic of Egyptian drawing.

The treatment of subjects in mass, with flat application of color, was resumed by the Coptic artisans, after the Greco-Roman interlude when they used the effects of perspective and modeling. Identical treatment was used on the two *orbiculi** in the "Nilometer"* (Louvre). In the medallion edged with red waves, the subjects stand out against a background of unbleached linen. The upper half comprises two seated gods: on the left the goddess Euthenia, who replaces the Egyptian goddess Isis, is surmounted by a black bird and holds a veil filled with flowers and fruits of the earth; on the right, the god Nile, who appears in Pharaonic Egypt under the

name of Hapi, is treated here in the Grecian style, in the pose assumed by the river or marine divinities of the Greco-Roman period. In the lower half, a *putto.** seated in a boat, catches a bird; another, equipped with scissors and a hammer, is busy climbing the column of a nilometer*, on the flooded banks of the Nile. These types of nilometers* appear from the period of the Later Roman Empire and consist of a graduated column in the center of a well, reached by a series of stairs. An identical scene is found at the

bottom of a silver casket dating from the beginning of the 6th century (Leningrad, Hermitage Museum).[2] The correct height of the flooding of the Nile is already engraved on the column by figures 17 and 18 (in cubits) inscribed in Greek. On the large statue of the god of the Nile in the Vatican which, in Isis' shrine in Rome, was the pendant of the figure of Tiber (mid 2nd century A.D.), the cubits are symbolized by sixteen little children playing around a semi-reclining god

Two tapestries, originally part of the same piece, are today preserved in two museums in the Soviet Union. The busts of the goddess Gaea and of the god Nile, bordered with crowns of flowers and foliage, are identified by an inscription and treated in a purely Greco-Roman style. The goddess Gaea, her hair in Libyan curls, is wearing a ringed solar disk on her head; her earrings are in the shape of uraei* while her coat, attached at her bosom by an Isis knot, partly conceals a vase or situle*. Here, the god-

Vase with dancer and stags
Tapestry and tabby. Linen and wool.
4-5th centuries
D. 24.5 cm
Leningrad, Hermitage Museum; inv. 11153
The composition of this fabric is similar to the piece conserved in Prague; however, the treatment of the vegetation, is handled more freely and the amorini are replaced by stags. In Christian iconography, these animals symbolize the catechumen preparing for baptism and are commonly used in decorating baptisteries; floor mosaics depict them, as in this example, quenching their thirst according to the description, in the first verses of psalm XLII.

Crux ansata
Tapestry. Linen and wool
5-7th centuries
46 x 30 cm
Paris, Musée du Louvre, Department of Egyptian Antiquities; inv. AF 5556
This textile is a convincing example of the Christianization of the crux ansata, "the sign of life" in pharaonic Egypt which enabled the gods to breath life into men and objects.

dess Isis, wife of Orisis, is replaced by the Greek goddess of the Earth and symbol of fertility and abundance. On the other medallion, Nile, in the guise of a bearded old man, holds a cornucopia; over his head is a large pink lotus.

The motif of a leafy tree full of birds, animals or people (Louvre; Museum of Decorative Arts, Prague; Hermitage) recalls the theme of birds in clumps of papyrus or trees with birds from Beni Hassa (Middle Egypt, Mid-Empire).

The archer Eros on a piece of textile in the Louvre[3] seems to have been copied from the hieroglyphic sign for the soldier; similarly, some of the dancers (Louvre)[4] resemble the hieroglyphic symbol for dancing.

The *ankh*, sign for life was often represented on Coptic objects because of its similarity with the sign

Orbiculus* **with nilometer***
Tapestry. Linen and wool
6th century
12.5 x 13.5 cm
Paris, Musée du Louvre,
Department of Egyptian
Antiquities ; inv. AF 5448
Two river gods, in the upper
part, assist in the
inscription of the Nile's
annual flood height on the
column of the nilometer*.
The style is still heavily
influenced by antique art,
but the modeling has
disappeared and given way
to flat colors. A flying
shuttle has been used to
trace the interior details.

of the cross. Aimed at infusing life into the gods and the dead (Fayum portrait, Louvre), it was deliberately adopted by the Christians because of the ancient prophecy that Christian cults would disappear when the hieroglyphic sign for "life" was worshipped (Rufin, Histoire Eccelésiastique, XI, 29). This accounts for the fact that the majority of Coptic monuments (stelae, artifacts, and daily objects) bear the ancient Egyptian sign for life. This vision is corroborated by the fact that on some textiles, the crux ansata is surrounded by the alpha and omega; sometimes, its loop even contains the chrisma or Grecian cross (Louvre ; Victoria and Albert Museum). Like stelae, the cross may be hung on the beak of a bird, a peacock or a dove, recalling the resurrection as in the "Crux ansata" in the Louvre. Moreover, this tapestry takes its name from the large crux ansata, where the loop is formed by a garland set with cabochons, enclosing two linked squares forming a star ; it is set between two columns whose capitals are decorated with a chrisma.

The juxtaposition of different time periods on an undivided register and the repeated appearances of the same figure, were methods of composition inherent in the Pharaonic tradition. The walls of temples and tombs are illustrated with all sorts of figures whose activities are shown in many small scenes, somewhat like a large book. Thus the textiles recounting the life of Joseph are presented as a series of small pictures, either horizontally or in circles, in which Joseph is dipicted with different people.

GRECO-ROMAN INFLUENCES

Greece and Rome were the initiators of a style and iconography in Egypt that completely renewed millenary traditions. Subjects taken from the repertory of classical mythology were preponderant throughout this period, which began with the founding of Alexandria in 332 B.C. The creation of this city, situated on a rocky isthmus between the sea and Lake Mariout, later to become one of the largest cities in the Greek world, marks the birth of a branch of Greek art, known as Alexandrian . The settling of Greek and Roman colonizers in the regional towns enabled the widespread diffusion of motifs throughout the country.

The Coptic textile weavers transformed the motifs and forms of other periods and places and gave them a special and distinctive look of their own.

In the Coptic period, the god Dionysus and his *thiase** are one of the preferred iconographical sources for all mediums. The cult of Dionysus, imported into Egypt by Alexander, was encouraged by the Ptolemies. To celebrate the New Year, Ptolemy II Philadelphia organized a large procession in honor of the triumph of Dionysus. Several Ptolemaic kings took the name of "Neos Dionysos" thereby ensuring the dynasty's divine legitimacy. The spread of this cult was facilitated by the early use of Dionysus to replace Osiris, the Egyptian god of the dead, resurrection and "master of the wine" mentioned in the Texts of the Pyramids. Dionysus' popularity was such that, as late as the end the 4th century A.D., the Greek pœt Nonnos, born at Panopolis (Akmin, Middle Egypt) still praised the glory of the god of wine in his *Dionysiacs* : "Speak, oh goddess, of breath which arouses the thunder of the son of Saturn, the nuptial spark which precedes the burning explosion and the lightning which was present at the union of Semele. Speak of the dual birth of Bacchus, whom Jupiter snatched still wet from the flames, the imperial product of an incomplete maternity." (Nonnos, *The Dionysiacs*, Song 1, 1-5)

The opening episode of the upper register of the "Voile d'Antinoé" is devoted to the childhood of Dionysus. This large printed veil was found in a humble tomb at Antinoopolis by Albert Gayet in 1905 : "This very important textile was used for packing ; it was twisted into rope and wrapped around the neck and arms of a poorly dressed woman, in order to keep the swaddling in the desired horizontal position."[5]

This veil, dating from the 4th century, was probably ordered by an association or rich property owner during a period of strong pagan reaction against the rise of Christianity. It may have later been considered uninteresting or worthless and was relegat-

ed to use in a tomb. The decoration is composed of two registers with figured scenes, separated by a frieze of foliage with birds. The upper register, missing several parts, illustrates the life-cycle of Dionysus. First of all, Semele is struck by a bolt of lightning. Next, the birth of Dionysus and Semele lying on her pallet surrounded by mid-wives while the child is bathed. According to mythology, Dionysus is born from Jupiter's thigh, after Semele is struck by lightning. Here, the birth is a natural one, in accordance with accounts by several writers of antiquity and illustrations on numerous sarcophagi and paintings. This iconography of the nativity and the bathing of the infant have often been compared, and quite justifiably, to the birth of Jesus. It is, in effect, a composition inherited from antique works, and was also used on a mosaic from Lebanon portraying the life of Alexander (4th century).[6] Pursued by the wrath of Hera, Dionysus is entrusted to the care of a silenus, seated on a rock covered with an animal skin. The warrior, wearing a helmet and brandishing a sword and shield, might be the personification of Envy who, in the guise of the god Mars, has come to stir up Hera's hatred. The final scene, from which large parts are missing, was probably devoted to the episode of Hermes delivering the young god to the care of the nymphs or the goddess Rhea. The large Bacchanalian procession of the lower register is comparable to processions depicted on sarcophagi or paintings showing troups of maenads, sileni, and stayrs dancing or playing music. Their style approaches the Bacchanalian figures decorating the silver Sassanian vases dating from the 4th century. Figures of this kind had a widespread influence through-out the Mediterranean in Roman times.

Dionysus, accompanied by Ariadne (?) appears in a statically composed tapestry of figures under individual arcades that are richly decorated with extremely varied vegetal and geometric motifs (Abegg Stiftung, Bern). The divine couple are surrounded by a peasant carrying a flail, a well-dressed woman, a woman undressing, Pan playing his pipes, and a satyr and maenad. The impressive dimensions of this incomplete tapestry (730 x 220 cm), along with the freshness of the colors and quality of work, divert us from the missing parts, and give us an overall vision of a piece that, until now, could not have been reassembled because of its dispersed fragments. Thus, the three fragments "Musical Maenad" (Bern), Dionysus (Museum of Fine Arts, Boston) and the "Maenad and Satyr" (Cleveland Museum of Art) analogous in style, iconography and composition, belong to the same piece.[7]

Dionysus appears triumphantly mounted on a chariot drawn by panthers in two instances in the

Dionysian procession
Detail : Noble woman
This personage is difficult to identify within the Dionysian context, the deceased? a personification? She is dressed in a tunic with an inset-band decorated with the ubiquitous foliage scrolls. An ample orange shawl with blue borders is draped around her back and over the shoulders. Similar to the Lady Theodosia found at Antinoopolis, her hair and ears are adorned with pearls.

Dionysian Procession
Tapestry and tabby. Linen and
wool
4th century
7.30 x 2.20 m
Bern (Riggisberg), Abegg Stiftung;
inv. 3100 a

The beginning of an arcade
on the extreme right
indicates that this piece was
originally larger and
probably centered on the

figures of Dionysus and
Ariadne. This piece is
stylistically and
iconographically similar to
all Dionysian figures which
date from the 4th century.

84

epic. Two exactly identical pieces of textile (Hermitage and Metropolitan Museum of Art) show him accompanied by Ariadne and by Hercules while a putto* (Eros?) drives the chariot. This concerns the last episode when the god discovers the sleeping Ariadne, who has been abandoned by Thesus on the Island of Naxos. This scene has been reproduced on numerous Roman sarcophagi.

After his victory over the Indians, Dionysus returned in a chariot surrounded by maenads, satyrs and prisoners (Hermitage;[7] Metropolitan Museum of Art[9]).This widespread imagery from the Roman world, is also found in a 4th century mosaic of a Syro-Egyptian fortress at Cheikh Zouede.[10]

The Dionysian cult is sometimes only referred to by the busts of Dionysus, Ariadne, maenads, nymphs, satyrs, Sileni, or Pan (Louvre; Metropolitan Museum of Art see page 89). The festivities surrounding the grape harvest was a favorite theme during Roman times, particularly the image of the grape-picking putti, that were fashionable in the 4th century (Louvre; Frühchristlich-byzantinische Sammlung, Berlin; Museum of Decorative Arts, Prague.) The success of these kinds of motifs is not only due to their funereal significance, for the harvesting of ripe fruit symbolizes the harvesting of human lives which have come to an end, but also to the idea of sacrifice followed by a resurrection, found in Christian thought. "I am the true vine and my father is the husbandman" (John, IV,1). This accounts for

Musical maenad
Tapestry and tabby. Linen and wool
4th century
1.43 x 0.855 m
Bern (Riggisberg), Abegg Stiftung; inv. 1637
Once part of set with the tapestries of the *"Maenad and Satyr"* (Cleveland Museum of Art) and the *"Dionysus"* (Boston Museum of Fine Arts), this piece depicts a maenad playing the lyre. The decor of this composition, imitating Roman Dionysian sarcophagi, consisted of several arcardes resting on columns, sheltering one or more characters from the *thiase**. A clearly sculptural effect, moreover, is added by color gradation.

Dionysus
Tapestry. Linen and wool
4th century
1.39 x 0.79 m
Boston, Museum of Fine Arts; inv. 1973.290
In accordance with traditional iconography, Dionysus, leaning against a column, holds a cornucopia in one hand and lifts his arms above his head. The two other fragments with which this forms a set *"Musical Maenad"* in Bern and *"Maenad and Satyr"* in Cleveland contain similar architectural traits: columns, architraves and coffered vaults.

Page 87 right :
Maenad and satyr
Tapestry. Linen and wool
4th century
1.39 x 0.857 m
Cleveland, Museum of Art ;
inv. 75.6
This fragment belongs to the
same set as the *"Musical
Maenad"* of Bern and the
"Dionysus" of Boston. The
same couple appear on the
Voile d'Antionoé (Musée du
Louvre) accompanied by
Greek inscriptions for wine
and wine-press.

Dionysian busts
Tapestry. Linen and wool
5-6th centuries
1.25 x 0.91 m
New York, Metropolitan Museum
of Art ; inv. 31.9.3
Dionysus's followers are
portrayed here in the form
of medallions recalling
mosaic pavements. The
larger fabric might have
been centered around
Dionysus, perhaps
accompanied by his wife
Ariadne, traditionally placed
at his side.

Rectangular panel with Dionysian decor.
Tapestry. Linen and wool
Akhmin? 4th century
34.9 x 21.9 cm
New York, The Metropolitan
Museum of Art; inv. 90.5.873.
Probably an ornament for
the front of a tunic, this
panel represents the
triumph of Dionysus after
his return from India. He is
depicted on a chariot drawn
by panthers and
is surrounded the members
of his *thiase**. The
background is formed of
vine shoots.

the fact that this theme is found on both Christian
and pagan sarcophagi (sarcophagus in San Lorenzo,
Rome, 3rd century; sarcophagus of the Good Shepherd, Latran Museum, Rome, 4th century.)

Hercules, one of the characters of the bacchanalian *thiase**, was often depicted in Coptic sculptures
and textiles. His powers against illness and thunder
made him a favorite motif on amulets. Some pieces
of material have a wide border framing a central motif. This border has been reserved for narration of
the Labors of Hercules. The central motif consists of
Dionysus and Ariadne in a chariot (Hermitage, Metropolitan Museum of Art). The twelve labors begin
at the top left hand corner: the lion of Nemea, the
golden apples of Hesperides, the wild boar of Ery-
manthus, the birds of the Stymphalian Marshes, the
bull of crete, Kyknos, Cerberus, the mares of
Diomedes, the augean stables, the Hydra of Lerna,

the wild hind of Arcadia and the girdle of the Queen
of the Amazons.

This last scene is reproduced in the central medallion of a textile in the Benaki Museum; at each
corner, diametrically identical scenes show the ab-
duction of Hercules' wife Deianeria by the centaur
Nessus, and Hercules attacking the centaur. On a
medallion (Coptic Museum, Cairo) the hero, seated
on a rock (?), struggles with the lion of Nemea, holding the beast by its mouth. A fragment of textile (Kanegafuchi Spinning Company, Kyoto) and a piece of
tunic (Louvre) depict Hercules pursuing a woman;
sometimes he brandishes a club, sometimes, in his
haste, it falls to the ground

The tunic from the Louvre is particularly precious
as its two yokes are decorated with a series of other
mythological scenes under blind arcades. In addition
to Hercules, the front also represents Perseus deliv-

**Vase with scenes of grape-
picking.**
Tapestry and tabby
Linen and wool
6th century
28.5 x 33 cm
Prague, Museum of Decorative
Arts ; inv. 1214

A vase with sprouting
plants is a current theme on
Coptic fabrics. If the plants
depicted are vines, the
branches are decorated with
animals or amorini
gathering grapes. On this
bichrome decor, a few traces
of color heighten the
subjects and convey an
effect of light on the somber
silhouettes treated by a
flying shuttle.

91

**Triumph of Dionysus
Tapestry. Linen and wool
6th century
22 x 21.5 cm**
Leningrad, Hermitage Museum;
inv. 11337
In the central medallion,
Dionysus and Ariadne ride a
chariot drawn by panthers.
Hercules appears at their
side, armed with a club. His
twelve labors are inscribed
on the tapestry frame in a
manner that recalls modern
comic strips. The funerary
significance of the Dionysian
and Herculean epics explain
their easy transition from
pagan to Christian
iconography.

ering Andromeda (?), Perseus and Athena, Aphrodite and Adonis (or Ares ?),and Narcissus, in front of
the nymph Echo, admiring himself in a fountain.The
episode of Perseus delivering Andromeda appears
on a square from the Manufacture Nationale des
Gobelins, in Paris ; images of Aphrodite and Adonis
(or Ares) have been treated at different periods in a
variety of styles (Elsa Bloch-Diener, Bern, 4th century see page 99 ; Louvre, 8th century).

Bellerophon, assisted by Pegasus, confronts the
Chimera on the central *orbiculus** of "Sabine shawl"
(Louvre, 6th century, see page 94).[11] According to
legend, the Chimera possessed the head of a lion,
body of a goat and tail in the shape of a snake. The
weaver has represented these details precisely, es-

pecially the goat's head on the monster's back. A
white ball outlined in black emerges from the Chimera's mouth ; this is undoubtedly the flame traditionally spewed by this mythical beast.

The right-hand square of the same shawl depicts
Apollo, arrested in his pursuit of Daphne,just as the
nymph changes into a laurel tree. However, before
disappearing, she offers him a flower in the form of
a cross, evidence perhaps of her Christian aspect.
The theme of Daphne turning into a laurel, appears,
moreover, several times on textiles and in stone
niches, as the symbol of transformation of the soul
after death.The left-hand square shows the goddess
Diana hunting lions with her bow, accompanied by
her favorite animal, the dœ. She appears in an iden-

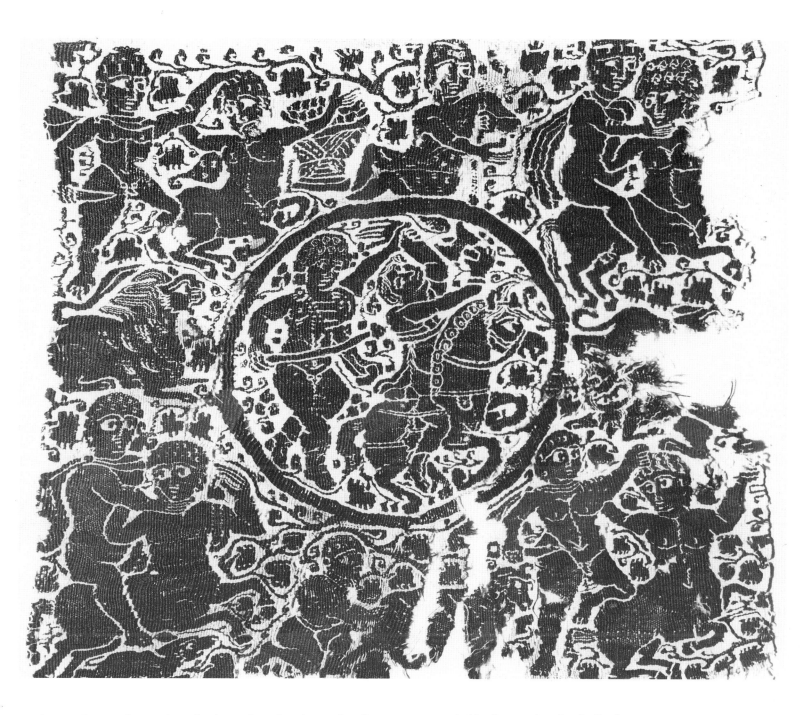

tical situation at the center of a large hanging in printed linen (Abegg Stiftung, 4th century)[12] surrounded by hunting heroes, some of whom are identified by inscriptions : Actaeon, Narcissus and Meleager.

A large, very fragmentary tapestry which dates from the same period represents a double arcature with a single pedestal upon which stands Atlantis and Meleager. The strong modeling of the figures is greatly influenced by the imperial sculptures from Lower Antiquity (Abegg Stiftung).[13] The two figures reappear in the 5th century on a tapestry in deep purple wool on a background of plain unbleached linen in "flat" colors (British Museum). Two large borders, as well as a central band, which separate the

two figures are occupied by figures dancing in the foliage or in an interlaced scroll design.

The hunt has always been a privileged theme in tapestries as an evocation of human force victorious over the animal world or the victory of the civilized over the savage. For example, the two archers, one battling with a boar and the other with a lion (Dumbarton Oaks Collection), reproduce the same schema as found on mural paintings (Bawit, Middle Egypt). Another hunter, with one knee on the ground, aided by his dog, pierces a beast with his lance (Louvre) ; this theme appears frequently in Roman mosaics. Pastoral representations, conceived in the same fashion as the large pavement mosaics from the Roman period (the Grand Palace in Constantinople,

Herculean cycle
Tapestry. Linen and wool
6th century
17 x 19.5 cm
Athens, Benaki Museum ; inv. 7035
In the center, Hercules seizes the magic belt from the queen of the Amazons. In two corners, the centaur Nessus abducts Hercules wife, Deianeira ; while in the other two corners, Nessus is killed by Hercules. The scene takes place against a background of grape vines, denoting the Dionysian character of Hercules.

"Sabine shawl"
Tapestry and tabby. Wool
Antinopolis ; 6th century
1.10 x 1.40 m
Paris, Musée du Louvre,
Department of Egyptian
Antiquities ; inv. E 29302
This piece was originally
decorated with four squares
surrounded by four galloons
at right angles. The center
of the shawl contains a large
medallion while flowers,
animals and *putti** are
strewn over a red ground.
This piece demonstrates the
strong attraction for
subjects taken from pagan
mythology during the
Christian period in Egypt.

Detail of the left square :
The huntress Diana,
accompanied by a dœ or a
dog (?), tramples on the lion
that she has just killed with
her arrow. This image, in
the "Coptic style",
reproduces the stance of the
famous statue of Diana by
the Greek sculptor
Leochares (4th century
B.C.).

Detail of the right square :
Depicted in the same stance
as his sister Diana, the god
Apollo gazes at the nymph
Daphne, who is being
transformed into a laurel.
She hands him a flower in
the form of a cross, which
might be construed as an
attempt to give the subject a
Christian content.

Detail of the central *orbiculus*
Bellerophon, aided by the
winged horse Pegasus, fights
the Chimera. The theme of
herœs in combat is derived
from 5th century B.C.
models in Greece. The so-
called "Nilotic" decoration on
the surrounding border
originates from the tradition
of aquatic scenes introduced
in Rome during the 1st
century A.D.

Orbiculus* with Hercules
Tapestry. Linen and wool
6th century
D. 10 cm
Cairo, Coptic Museum; 7689
Hercules, armed with his
club, fights the Nemean
Lion. This medallion belongs
to a set of fabrics with dark
decoration on undyed linen
which imitated the Roman
black and white mosaics.

Hercules chasing a maenad
Tapestry. Linen and wool
5th century
Osaka, Kanegafuchi Spinning
Company
Hercules, bearing a club,
chases a maenad who holds
onto her wind-filled veil.
The same theme is
illustrated, in a different
style, on the yoke in the
Musée du Louvre (E 29294).

**Collar ornament of a tunic
Tapestry. Linen and wool
Antinoopolis; 3rd century
35 x 15 cm**
Paris, Musée du Louvre,
Department of Egyptian
Antiquities; inv. E 29294
The presence of diverse
mythological subjects in the
decoration of this collar
shows the persistence of
customs which the religious
authorities must have had
difficulty in eradicating. The
piece faithfully reproduces
the iconography and style of
the mosaics and sculptures
of the 3rd century with
which it was undoubtedly
contemporary.

Aphrodite and Adonis
Tapestry. Linen and wool
3-4th centuries
22.8 x 23.5 cm
Bern, Elsa Bloch-Diener, Antike
Kunst
The two lovers are
portrayed *contrapposto*, a
posture typical of statuary.
The medallion is integrated
in a band with linear
decoration which constrasts
with the central motif. The
flying shuttle dominates.

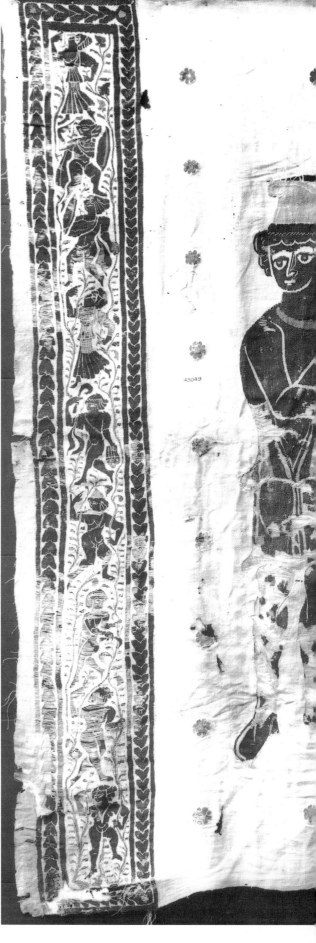

Artemis
Resist printed linen
Ashmunein; 4th century
6 x 1.94 m
Bern (Riggisberg), Abegg Stiftung;
inv. 1397
Artemis stands in a stepped
edicula, signifying that the
sanctuary houses the statue
of the goddess. The vast
composition, organized
around the goddess, groups,
on the left, four
mythological heroes
(Actaeon, Narcissus,
Meleager, and Adonis) and
offers, on the right, hunting
scenes on two levels. The
technique of resist printing,
which appears to be
typically Egyptian, can
without generalizing
guarantee the provenance of
the majority of such fabrics.

Meleager and Atalanta
Tapestry and tabby. Linen and
wool
5th century
2 x 1.5 m
London, British Museum;
inv. 43049
This piece portrays the two
characters from Greek
mythology in a style that is
completely different from
that of the 4th century
tapestry in the Abegg
Stiftung in Riggisberg.

4th century) or as seen in illustrated manuscripts, were a common theme on Coptic textiles and presented scenes of various origins, sometimes reassembled in a single composition. The literary tradition of pastoral poetry which began with the Idylls of the Greek poet Theocritus (around 315-250 B.C.) and followed by the Ecologues of Virgil (70-19 B.C.) seems to have been particularly treasured in the 5th and 6th centuries. The four medallions in the Brooklyn Museum form an unexpected iconographic ensemble; some scenes are also reproduced on silver plates, sarcophagi or other textiles. The first represents a seated woman breast-feeding her child, a shepherd pulls a bucket from a well as two cows drink, an old shepherd leaning on his staff and a flock of sheep. In the second, a young shepherd, surrounded by his flock and his dog, offers a lamb to an old man seated in front of a hut, a seated woman plays with her child, one shepherd plays his flute while another shepherd kills a snake which is wrapped around a tree, with his axe. On the third medallion, a shepherd lies on the ground with a dog, a shepherdess carries her child on her back and drives a flock of sheep and goats towards a seated old man who is leaning on his staff. The fourth shows three men feasting while two dogs await their share, a servant skins an animal hanging from a tree while another makes a fire under a cauldron; these last two figures are separated by a large bowl (of wine?).

A square from the Saint Louis Museum and a medallion from the Louvre both show a scene of a goat being milked. In both examples, a shepherd crouches behind the animal and pours milk into a bucket. Another medallion (Louvre) shows a seated peasant throwing grain to hens.

Figures of dancers and musicians are added to the Dionysian and pastoral settings but these figures are also frequently found in isolated decorations. The figure of the dancer is particularly interesting in that the evolution of the schema can be followed across an entire period. The "classic" dancers on the tunic (Pushkin Museum) or on the "Voile d'Antinoé" (Louvre, 4th century), are very close stylistically to the "Alexandrine" ivories (3rd-4th centuries) which were made to ornament furniture. During the 5th century, the dancers became stylized (Louvre; Abegg Stiftung) though preserving their naturalistic forms until the 7th century (dancer's head, Louvre) but during the 8th century the bodies become dislocated so that by the 12th century, the original is represented by a "sign" consisting of a square head attached to two raised arms and two legs (Louvre).

Other textiles depict dancers wielding crotalae*, castanets or cymbals, accompanied by musicians playing flutes, panpipes and lyres. These scenes often show a young woman being serenaded (Coptic Museum, Cairo; Brooklyn Museum, Abegg Stiftung; Louvre). The Musée Georges Labit in Toulouse owns a large piece of linen containing two identical med-

Square with hunter
Tapestry. Linen and wool
6th century
9.5 x 9 cm
Paris, Musée du Louvre,
Department of Egyptian
Antiquities; inv. E 17368
In this carefully treated composition, a hunter and his dog are presented within a frame of amphora and bowls containing vine branches. All of these elements are handled in flat tones and highlighted by the use of flying shuttle.

allions. The Louvre possesses a fragment of one of the medallions which, when superimposed on the Toulouse piece, permits the almost complete reconstruction of the textile[14] (see page 112). Two figures, encircled by a border, appear against a red background; the male figure, dressed in green, and wearing a gold headband, plays a lyre; the female figure, dressed in a white and ochre tunic, with a green scarf, drapes her arm around the shoulder of her companion. On the Toulouse fragment, she raises a circular golden object. The composition is identical to that of a carved stone niche in the Coptic Museum in Cairo,[15] often identified as either an Orpheus and Eurydice or David and Melody. This piece has also been called a Judgement of Paris because of the golden "apple" held by the woman. However, the object being held by the female figure might also be a castanet, like those seen in the dancers on the piece from the Louvre, in which case it might then be identified as a satyr and maenad.

Episodes from Homer's poems were often used by weavers. A Judgement of Paris (Textile Museum, Washington D.C.) depicts the young man in conversation with the three goddesses. In the lower part, Athena leans on a shield and holds a round object in one hand; on the left, Hera, wearing a veil and a long chiton*, holds a round object, divided into four segments. These objects, which are obviously being offered to Paris, might symbolise, the sovereignty over Asia promised by Hera and the victory in battle

Orbiculus* in a rural theme
Tapestry. Linen and wool
7th century
7 x 6.5 cm
Paris, Musée du Louvre,
Department of Egyptian
Antiquities; inv. AF 5675
This *orbiculus** is part of a series of rural subject that were very popular during the Coptic period.

Collar decorated with rural motifs
Tapestry. Linen and wool
5-6th centuries
35.5 x 7 cm
Paris, Musée du Louvre,
Department of Egyptian
Antiquities; inv. AF 5512
Scenes from rural life, such as these goatherds guarding their flock were wide-spread "cliches" in the Roman world.

Four *orbiculu representing
bucolic scenes**
Tapestry. Wool
Antinoopolis? 5-6th centuries
11.9 x 12.1 cm 12.2 x 10.9 cm
11.9 x 11.5 cm 11.8 x 11.5 cm
New York, Brooklyn Museum;
inv. 44.143 (A-D)
These pieces can be
compared with other textiles
and *artifacts* depicting
everyday rural life in
anitiquity. The models for
these kinds of scenes came
from literary descriptions
and miniatures, reproduced
until the Middle Ages.

Preceding page :
Pastoral scene
Tapestry. Linen and wool
Akhmin ? 5-6th centuries
34.3 x 33.7 cm
Saint Louis, The Saint Louis Art
Museum ; inv. 48.1939
The composition of the
tapestry into four trapezoids
surrounding a square
creates a trompe-l'œil effect
in imitation of the cover of a
jewellery box (the gilded-
silver Projecta jewellery box
in the British Museum,
London)

Orbiculus* in rural motifs
Tapestry. Linen and wool
7th century
8.5 x 8.5 cm
Paris, Musée du Louvre,
Department of Egyptian
Antiquities ; inv. AF 5445
This picturesque scene of
daily life reproduced on
textile was proably based on
a "cartoon" from a pattern-
book used for moasics and
paintings.

Page 108 above :
Square of dancers
Tapestry. Linen and wool
6th century
15 x 14.4 cm
Paris, Musée du Louvre,
Department of Egyptian
Antiquities ; inv. AF 5607
The theme of the dancer,
whether depicted alone, in
couples or in processions, is
a leitmotif on Coptic fabrics.
The stylistic evolution and
progressive abstraction of
this motif can be followed
through to the 12th century.

Page 108 below :
Square with dancers
Tapestry. Linen and wool
8-9th centuries
25.3 x 23.5 cm
Paris, Musée du Louvre,
Department of Egyptian
Antiquities ; inv. AF 5947
The stylized foliage scrolls
that form a frieze of
juxtaposed medallions, the
outer border of crenellated
motifs and the arrangement
of the figures are all
characteristic traits of the
Arab period.

Page 109 :
Front of a tunic
Tapestry. Linen and wool
9th century
55.5 x 42 cm
Paris, Musée du Louvre,
Department of Egyptian
Antiquities ; inv. AF 5573
This tunic was decorated
with a profusion of dancers,
either facing front or with
the head completely tilted
back.

promised by Athena. The kneeling Aphrodite, personifying beauty, is eventually chosen by Paris. The theme and pose of Aphrodite bathing (Musée de Cluny; Louvre, p. 114-115), dating from the Hellinistic period, will be taken up by artists throughout succeeding centuries, in a diversity of mediums.

The Hermitage[16] and The Boston Museum of Fine Arts[17] each hold matching medallions representing the Judgement of Paris. Against a red background bordered with wave motifs, this particular Judgement of Paris shows Zeus enthroned in the upper part. At his side is Paris, dressed in oriental clothing, while a nude Hermes (identifiable by his winged feet) flies towards the king of the gods. In the lower part, Aphrodite, holding a veil in her hands, is flanked by Hera, on the left and by Athena, wearing some sort of headdress, on the right.

Three succeeding episodes of the illiad (18, 368, 616) are condensed in "Thetis in Hephaestus' forge" (Victoria and Albert Museum, p. 116). The episodes

include Thetis in the forge of Hesphaetus, Hesphaetus forging weapons and Thetis giving the weapons to Achilles. The textile shows the god of the forge seated in front of Thetis while Achilles tries on the armor. A shield bearing a profile might symbolize a deified Achilles acceding to immortality –a condition that would be shared by the deceased owner of the tissue.

A medallion from Frankfurt (p. 116) based on Euripides *Iphigenia*, recounts the moment when Iphigenia is about to sacrifice Orestes and Pulades. The central section contains a statue of Artemis in an arrangement that is similar to that found in the "Sabine shawl." On the left, the priestress Iphigenia, flourishes the sacrificial knife while entreating King Thoas. The king, armed with a shield, replies with the same gesture. He is dressed in trousers or leggings and wears a Phyrigian bonnet that denotes his barbarian origins. In the lower part, the victims

kneel on either side of the altar of fire, with their hands tied behind their backs.

A Rape of Europa and Pasihae and the bull (Brooklyn Múseum, p. 117) attest to the varied use of Greek mythology; while allegorical figures like the Three Graces (Louvre, p. 117) or the Seasons (Louvre; British Museum) represent nature's fertility and the passage of time.

The heads of the Seasons appear on fragments of "bouclé" textiles as young curly haired men with crowns of leaves, fruit or flowers. The same faces are reproduced in the lower corners of the weaving, "Putti in a boat" (British Museum) which indicates the valued position initially held by these fragments, now dispersed in numerous museums and collections. A mosaic of the Seasons found in a villa at Daphne, near Antioch (Louvre, 5th century)[18] and two orbiculi in the Louvre (4th century) present the Seasons as young women, each identified by Greek inscriptions as Winter and Spring. Their half-length portraits are also represented on textiles. Winter is dressed in a hooded coat. In one hand she holds a vase with handles and, in the other, a stick from which hangs a duck. The figure of Spring is holding a stick covered with blossoms.

Central scenes are frequently framed with groups of gesticulating *putti** or nereids with wind-blown veils often seated on sea monsters. This theme, derived from marine compositions, may also occupy the principal place on vast hangings of sumptuous colors. The weaving (Dumbarton Oaks Collection) of two large nereids on a bright red background is just one example. One black-haired nereid is placing a garland around the neck of a sea animal which has the head of a bull, while the blonde nereid is shown admiring herself in a mirror which reflects her image. A rich frame, bordered with festoons of pomegranates, is covered with a foliated scroll full of birds. Another weaving, also in Washington (the Textile Museum, 5th-6th centuries) has a red background overflowing with motifs and conveying the same "covered" impression as a carpet. A nereid in each corner and a fifth one in the center form the basic design around which the other elements are organized : *putti**, birds, fish and vegetation so that no place is left uncovered. The frame is filled with winged horses (Pegasus?) separated by trees with two branches.

The goddess most closely associated with water is the Goddess of Love, Aphrodite, born from sea foam (anadyomene). She is represented standing in a shell, rising up from a wave, supported by nereids or tritons (Louvre); two *putti** help the goddess who is wringing out her hair. This "classic" presentation of a theme in Antiquity and on Coptic sculptures (Lou-

*Orbiculus** with Aphrodite
Anadyomene
**Tapestry and tabby. Linen and
wool**
6th century
D. 11 cm
Paris, Musée de Cluny ; inv. 22453
Aphrodite is depicted on a
ground of unbleached linen
and black wool. The
crouching goddess wrings
her tresses as she leaves her
bath. This theme was
created during the
Hellenistic period and is still
handled in a very classical
manner in this medallion.

Fragment of a tunic
**Tapestry and tabby. Linen and
wool.**
6th century
79.7 x 19 cm
Paris, Musée du Louvre,
Department of Egyptian
Antiquities ; inv. AF 5558

This square of Aphrodite
Anadyomene, surrounded by
nereids, was originally part
of the shoulder of the tunic.
The same design would have
been repeated on the other
half of the garment.

Thetis in Hephaestus's forge
Tapestry. Linen and wool
6th century
12.7 x 12.7 cm
London, Victoria and Albert
Museum ; inv. 2140-1900
Two scenes are condensed
into one : Thetis' visit to
Hephaestus and the forging
of Achilles' arms. The
interior details of the black
silhouettes are highlighted
in unbleached linen by
flying shuttle technique.

Orbiculus* Iphigenia in Taurus
Tapestry. Linen, wool and silk
6th century
D. 12.6 cm
Frankfurt am Main, Museum für
Kunsthandwerk ; inv. 3610
This *orbiculus** belongs to a
restricted series that
attemps to reproduce
mythological scenes in the
style of black and white
Roman mosaics from the 1st
to 3rd centuries A.D.

Orbiculus* Pasiphae (?) and a bull
Tapestry. Linen and wool
Antinoopolis; 4-7th centuries
D. 10 cm
New York, Brooklyn Museum;
inv. 15429
This scene might also represent Europa seduced by Zeus who has been transformed into a bull. The naked figure seen from the back is reminiscent of Greco-Roman art.

Orbiculus* of Three Graces
Tapestry. Linen and wool
6-7th centuries
D. 9.5 cm
Paris, Musée du Louvre, Department of Egyptian Antiquities; inv. AF 5433
The famous dance of the three graces, created in the late 4th or early 3rd centuries B.C., is here depicted by disproportionate figures resulting from the use of the flying shuttle.

vre)[19] which in the same manner as Aphrodite in the bath, reappears constantly on much later monuments (*The Birth of Venus*, Botticelli, 15th century).

Like Aphrodite, Christ was considered a pearl born from an oyster. While, however, it is difficult to prove that the theme of Aphrodite's birth was christianized, it does seem very likely that the association of Christ with a pearl goes back to the birth of Aphrodite.

Treated as an icon, such as the enthroned Virgin or Christ in Bawit and Saqqara, the personification of fire and hearth, the goddess Hestia Polyolbos ("Hestia the Bountiful"), is seated on a throne ornamented with pearls and cabochons (Dumbarton Oaks Collection, 6th century). On a background of vegetation, six *putti** advance towards Hestia; each is offering her a medallion inscribed with the words "Wealth", "Joy", "Praise", "Abundance", "Virtue" and "Progress". The two large female figures framing the central group, one of whom holds a casket (?) upon which the inscription, "light", is still visible, occupy the place of the angels on Christian representations.

Through these myths, personifications and symbols, Greco-Roman imagery created, all around the Mediterranean, a tradition founded on a moral order that could easily fit into a Christian interpretation.

ORIENTAL INFLUENCES

If the silk textiles found in Egypt must have been woven in the Orient and, in particular, in Persia Sassanide*, it is more difficult to make the same as-

sertion for weavings in wool or linen which present iconographic analogies with the Orient. The pentagonal leaves placed in staggered rows on the cushion covers (Louvre) incline to the right or the left according to a typically Oriental schema.

The same motifs are found in the repertory of Oriental textiles as well as in Byzantine and Coptic textiles double palmettos, flower motifs which fill all available space, pairs of wings with curved ends, animals, such as winged horses and human heads arranged in staggered lines (The Textile Museum; Musée Historique des Tissus). Several weavings have frames of red flowers with four petals, either open or in profile. This sort of flower is common on Sassanide* art objects and is found throughout the Mediterranean basin; examples from 6th century Ravenna on mosaics, vaults and clothing (Theodora's Cortege, San Vitale)[21] attest to its widespread popularity.

The eagle with its head turned, holding a crown in his beak, is seen on several tapestries (Louvre tican Museum; Berlin Museum). It appears on Sassanide* cloth, silk goods from Antinoopolis and Coptic fabrics (parrots, stags, ibex)[22] wearing a pearl necklace with two ribbons streaming out behind.

Animals facing some feature of vegetation (Jonas tapestry, Louvre) evoke the theme, well-known in the Orient, of animals situated on either side of the "Tree of Life".

On two pieces of woven textile (Louvre; Musée Historique des Tissus), believed to be leggings (pieces of clothing of Oriental origin) the field is occupied by a battle scene between horsemen-archers and foot soldiers; in the center, a Sassanide* king seated on a throne is either a copy from a Sassanide textile or, more probably, from the decoration on a silver or gold cup.[23]

While there are few references to Oriental myths in this classic context, the diffuse penetration of motifs enriches, in new and sometimes singular ways, pagan and Christian repertories.

CHRISTIAN ICONOGRAPHY

This is the setting in which the new religion, originally from the Orient, spread to the countries bordering the Mediterranean.

The beginning of the Old Testament is illustrated on a textile in the Victoria and Albert Museum by two nude figures separated by a column; they can be identified as Adam and Eve[24] according to a schema identical to paintings (dome of the Chapel of Peace, Bagauat, 5th century).[25] The other themes refer to the prophets or patriarchs who prefigure Christ.

The best and most widely represented of these

Panel with two nereids
Tapestry. Linen and wool
5-6th centuries
1.44 x 0.82 m
Washington D.C., Dumbarton Oaks
Collection ; inv. 32.1
The theme of nereids,
although customary on
Roman and Coptic artifacts,
is astonishingly rejuvenated
here by the weaving
technique and by the
isolation of the figures on a
magnificent red ground.

Nereid
Limestone
Herakleopolis Magna (Ahnas)
Beginning of the 5th century
H. 60 cm. L. 52 cm
Trieste, Museo Civico ; inv. 5620
These two nereids are
characterized by the
schematic treatment of the
bodies and the poorly
individualized faces. The
rigid veils encircling their
heads are stylistically far
removed from the fluid
draperies of the Greco-
Roman period. The central
putto*, straddling a dolphin
and playing the crotala,
places this scene in the
aquatic environment of
Nilotic representations. The
arched form of the superior
egg-and-dart border,
indicates that the piece
consists of a conch broken at
the two extremities. The
central mask is a current
iconographical theme on
Roman sarcophagi.

The birth of Aphrodite
Tapestry. Linen and wool
6th century
27 x 26 cm
Paris, Musée du Louvre, Department of Egyptian Antiquities ; inv. AF 5470
The image of Aphrodite Anadyomene in a conch shell,
supported by a triton and nereid and flanked by sea divinities
is inherited from reliefs of the Roman period.

themes is the figure of Joseph, son of Jacob; the special quality of the representation appears in a cyclical treatment.[26] The relevant textiles belong to a homogeneous series characterized by the use of red backgrounds against which the figures in light colors stand out clearly; they are often in yellow tones, highlighted by the blue or green color of their clothing. The borders are made up of lines of cordiform leaves or stylized foliated scrolls encircled by two bands of cabochons in different colors. The style of compact bodies whose shapes begin to be dislocated and square-shaped, open eyes suggests a date for these tapestries in the 7th or 8th century.[27] Certain examples have rectangular bands with two registers interrupted in the center by a medallion (Pushkin Museum; Louvre). Others have a circular arrangement of scenes around a central medallion (Krefeld Museum; Metropolitan Museum of Art; Pushkin Museum; Musée de Trèves; Louvre; Museum of Tarrasa; Kanegafuchi Spinning Company; Museum of Decorative Arts). A tunic fragment in the Museum of Northern Bohemia, Liberec, has two wide galloons which terminate with two medallions illustrated with scenes from the life of Joseph. The vertical arrangement of this design makes it somewhat difficult to read. The central medallion has two different themes, either Joseph's dream according to Genesis

Gallon decorated with bacchic themes
Tapestry. Linen and wool
5th century
1.47 x 0.26 m
Paris, Musée du Louvre, Department of Egyptian Antiquities; inv. AF 5511
The border and flowers of the frame are identical to the *Shawl of vines* (see page 56). The five figures, belonging to the bacchic thiase*, appear like "shadowgraphs" and are outlined by the use of flying shuttle. One of the figures holds a double-headed axe, symbolizing sacrifice and signifying the foreign origin of the bacchic cult.

Tunic
Tapestry and tabby. Linen and wool
11th century
63 x 85.5 cm
Paris, Musée du Louvre, Department of Egyptian Antiquities; inv. E. 26299
During the Byzantine period, clothing covered in woven flowers were usually worn by emperors, important dignitaries and religious figures.

123

37.9, "I have dreamed a dream more; and, behold, the sun and the moon and the eleven stars made obeisance to me." or, the voyage by camel of Joseph and an Ishmaelite to Egypt. The scenes on the large medallions read from the upper zone to the left or to the right. On the Treves textile the cycle is read counter-clockwise: Jacob sends Joseph to his brothers; Joseph is with his brothers; he is pulled out of the cistern (into which he had plunged); Joseph's coat is drenched with the blood of a goat; Joseph is sold to the Ishmaelites (foreshadowing the selling of Christ by Judas); Reuben, one of Joseph's brothers, laments in front of the empty cistern; the voyage of Joseph and an Ishmaelite to Egypt; Joseph is sold to Potiphar, a eunuch of the Pharaoh and captain of the guards (Genesis 37, 12-36).

The same scenes are reproduced on the rectangular bands but are curiously cut by the central motif (Pushkin Museum). The figure of Joseph seems to have been particularly valued in the Jewish and Christian circles in Egypt. Close iconographic comparisons can be established with the silk cloths from this period (Sens cathedral, 5th-6th centuries)[28] and the ivory throne of Maximilien (Museo Arcivescovile, Ravenna, 6th century).[29] Nevertheless, both go back to an iconographic tradition illustrated by manuscripts, for example, the Genesis by Cotton (British Library Board, 6th century).[30]

Though widely represented in the Early Christian and Christian world, two textiles recount the history of the prophet Jonas. He is also represented on two Egyptian monuments (painting, chapel of Exodus, Bagauat, 4th century;[31] sculpture, Bawit, Louvre, 6th century).[32] Like Joseph, however, his popularity (because he was compared to Christ) was such that he was often represented to evoke the burial and resurrection of Christ (Matthew, XII, 39-40). In most instances, the cycle is composed of three episodes: Jonas is thrown into the sea and swallowed by the whale; the creature rejects him; the prophet rests under the cucurbitacaea. The central episode appears on the Louvre tapestry (5th-6th centuries): Jonas, kneeling in prayer, surges forth from the creature's mouth against a woven background of foliage of cucurbitacaea and gourds; his name is inscribed above his head. On a printed cloth composed of three registers (Cleveland Museum, 5th century),[33] Jonas rests under the cucurbitacaea following the pose adopted by the young shepherd, Endymion. The whale's tail is at his feet, a reminder probably of the preceding scene.

A textile previously preserved in the Königliche Kunstgewerbemuseum in Berlin, unfortunately fragmentary, shows Daniel between the lions. Sumptuously dressed in a short oriental tunic, a coat and leggings entirely covered with circular and cross motifs, wearing a Phrygian hat, he is in a praying position between two crouching lions, their heads facing backwards. On the right, the prophet Habakkuk carries a dish with a bowl and bread sent by God for the starving Daniel who has been locked up for seven days in the lion pit by the Persian King Cyrus. The theme, a common one since the period of the catacombs, is often reduced to the sole figure of Daniel between the lions (wooden console, Bawit(?), 5th century, Berlin Staatliche Museen).[35] Habakkuk appears sporadically either close to Daniel as seen on this textile, or in the air, which conforms to the biblical text (Daniel 14, 35-36). On the other hand, the upper and lower borders are particularly worthy of attention; they are occupied by two series of small temples, identified by the inscriptions to a church and to the martyrs (the site of a cult consecrated to the martyr saints) dedicated to the saints, such as, Michael, Stephen, Suzanne.

The sacrifice of Isaac appears on three identical textiles which are probably part of the same group (Musée Historique des Tissus; Walters Art Gallery; New York Cooper Union Museum). Abraham, the father of Isaac brandishes a two-edged sword in one hand and grasps the boy by the hair with the other. The nude boy kneels on the circular sacrificial altar which is decorated with blue and yellow tiles. Under Abraham's feet is the ram which will replace the child on the altar. According to Genesis XXII, 13, the animal was caught by his horns in a bush: the foliage is in front of Abraham's face while the trunk, hidden by the patriarch's body, twists along to the ram's horns. Appearing out of the clouds, evoked by a blue ribbon, the hand of the angel stops Abraham as he prepares to kill his son: "Lay not thine hand upon the lad, neither do thou any thing unto him,..." (Genesis XXII, 12). If Abraham symbolizes the obedience to God, Isaac who has carried the faggots for this own sacrifice can be compared to Christ carrying his cross. Contrary to the Jonas theme, this theme was widely dispersed throughout Egypt on paintings and sculptures. A third textile (Abegg Stiftung), unfortunately missing many sections, can, by its looped technique and style, be linked with the Jonas weaving at the Louvre (?). The preserved piece indicates, at least, the existence of four iconographic registers situated between two pilasters of tree trunks and capitals covered with geometric motifs. The second register, beginning at the bottom, represents the sacrifice of Isaac though all that remains of this scene is the base of the altar, the feet and an arm of Abraham and the ram perched in a tree. The more static treatment of the scene and the staircase-form of the altar suggest an association

Orbiculus **representing the life
of Joseph
Tapestry. Linen and wool
8th century
29.5 x 28 cm**
Trier, Stadtmuseum ; inv. 17

A homogeneous series of
fabrics retrace the life of the
patriarch Joseph according
to a narrative cycle, probably
modeled on an illustrated
manuscript.

with the painting of Saqqara (Convent of Saint Jeremy, 6th century) and also with an ivory pyxide* (Staatliche Museen, 6th century).[38]

Just beneath an Ascension of Elijah, unique in the Coptic monuments, is Elijah, presented in traditional fashion in a chariot of fire. About to be raised up to the sky, he holds his mantle out to Elisha, while the hand of God appears from the clouds to draw him up. The names of the persons are inscribed at the level of the heads. It is surprising that this theme has not been more frequently represented either in Egypt or in Christian art. The comparison of the Ascension of Elijah with Christ's Ascension seems inevitable. On the other hand, at the time of the Transfiguration, Elijah's appearance with Moses next to Christ, represents the order of the prophets.

On the textiles in the Cleveland Museum of Art and the ; Victoria and Albert Museum,[39] Moses receives the Tablets of the Law. On the Cleveland piece, this scene is associated with the vision of the Burning Bush but the voice of Yahweh is replaced by the figure of Christ.

In this way, the parallel between the Old and New Testament is established not only by the texts but also in art works, which evidently includes textiles.

Following the order of the Gospels, the first scene opens with the Annunciation,one on a silk-embroidered cloth and another printed (Victoria and Albert Museum).[40] The Proclamation of the Virgin's Divine Maternity at the Council of Ephesus in 431 has probably given a strong impetus to the elaboration of a Marian iconography. According to the Apocryphus, the Virgin was seated spinning the "purple" for the Temple veil when the Archangel Gabriel came to make his announcement.[41] In this ancient iconography, the Virgin is on the left and Gabriel on the right according to a schema which was common during this period (Annunciation, wood, 5th century Louvre).[42]

On the embroidered medallion, the Annunciation accompanies the Visitation scene : the Virgin and Saint Elizabeth are tenderly embracing. On a woven textile from the same museum the position of the two embracing women also gives the impression of a Visitation,[43] a representation also found on an embroidered *clavus* at the Musée de Cluny in Paris.

The Nativity is reproduced on a printed textile (Victoria and Albert Museum) and also on an embroidered cloth (Louvre). One fabric has a horizontal arrangement while the other is vertical. The difference is probably due to the use of fabrics, probably a hanging mural for the printed textile, perhaps a piece of clothing for the embroidered textile. There are two different models for the same scene ; the first is of Greco-Roman origin, the second shows Byzantine influence. The Virgin seated on a couch with an angel seems to be a copy of the Nativity of Dionysus reproduced on the "Voile d'Antinoé" (Louvre). We see the same position of the Virgin and Semele, the same type of bed with slats and feet marked by engraved crosses, the same position of the angel and the servant at the head of the bed, the same cup placed under the bed. Many details are found in the two images whose relationship is also confirmed by the printing technique. In front of the Virgin, though unfortunately fragmentary, is the creche with the Infant, overlooked by the cow and donkey.

The arrangement of the figures and the treatment of the subject in embroidery goes back to the Palestinian model passed on through the Byzantine world. The Virgin is lying on a couch in the form of an oval mattress. The episode takes place at the instant when, according to the Apocryphal Gospels, the mid-wife Salome, incredulous at Mary's virginity, watches her hand dry up.[45] On this cloth, as well as on the ivory chair of Maximilien at Ravenna (6th century),[46] the mid-wife's hand is depicted disproportionately large as though to emphasize the miracle. Joseph is seated at the Virgin's feet, one hand on his cheek. Above the group, the Infant rests in the crib surmounted by the cow, the donkey and two angels. The same vertical composition is also found on a volet of a Coptic icon (Golenishchev Collection, 6th-7th centuries) ;[47] the same iconographic type is found on the ampullae from the Holy Land and on the later Byzantine icons.

The Adoration of the Magi (or shepherds) is reproduced on three textiles with different techniques : a printed textile (Cleveland Museum of Art, 5th century),[48] a piece of embroidery (Victoria and Albert Museum, 5-6th centuries),[49] and several tapestries (Private collection, Paris, 7-8th centuries, British Museum).[50] The Virgin, holding the child on her knees, is always seated on the left.On the printed textile, the three kings bearing gifts, advance eagerly toward the group. They are dressed in boots and leggings, short tunics and Phrygian hats,a typically oriental style of dress, commonly worn by kings or holy figures (Daniel, The Three Hebrews). The composition which is spread horizontally and the rapid movement of the Magi, seems to be the replica of the same scene decorating sarcophagi, artifacts (Capsella from Brivio, Louvre, 5th century), and, in particular, the lower part of the coat of Empress Theodora (mosaic, San Vitale, Ravenna), where two of the three Magi are clearly visible. The poor state of the embroidery, makes it difficult to decipher. Nevertheless, there are still vestiges of the chair, where Mary is usually seated, as well as the

legs of two people (Magi or shepherds). The tapestry medallions, stylistically close to the medallion in the Joseph-cycle, present a circular composition, with the Virgin and child situated on the lower left, and the Magi, accompanied by an angel (?) creating the form of a circle. It is possible that the printed textile in Cleveland represents the baptism of Christ. Effectively, the only remaining figure is that of St. John offering his hand to another person wearing a halo (Christ), who has almost entirely disappeared. A unique example on textiles from Egypt,this theme has been frequently illustrated since the Early Christian period for, through this act, Christ was specifically designated as the Son of God. "This is my beloved Son in whom I am well pleased" (Matthew, 3, 13-17)

Another unique example is found in the representation of the Last Supper on an embroidered medallion in the Victoria and Albert Museum.[51] The remaining section shows nine of the apostles seated around a semi-circular table, known as a sigma. The apostles are shown in a reclining position, traditionally found in antiquity ; a servant bearing an amphora, approaches the table already laid with a plate of fish and nine loaves. This episode was introduced at a later date (6th century) and bears the distinct mark of Byzantine influence (mosaic of S. Apollinare Nuovo, Ravenna, 6th century ; Massano Gospel, 6th century).

Despite A. Kendrick's interpretation of the iconography of the two embroidered medallions as an Adoration of the Magi,[52] and as an Angel announcing the Resurrection of Our Lord to Mary Magdalene[53](Victoria and Albert Museum), another hypothesis seems possible. One of the medallions shows three holy figures standing close together, with a hand on their chest and the other on their stomachs ; a fourth person stands in front of them, who seems to be pointing to something that has now disappeared. Given their ample garments, their veiled heads, their static pose and empty hands, it would seem more probable to recognize them as Holy Women at the Tomb rather than Magi. On the other hand, the presence of Christ with a cruciferous halo on the second piece excludes it from being a The announcement of the Resurrection . A standing figure, accompanied by an angel pointing out the scene, turns his gaze towards Christ. A smaller figure with his hand towards the body of Christ, can be glimpsed between the former two figures. Could this be the Doubting of Saint Thomas ?

The miracles of Christ are recognizable on two printed textiles. The Miracle of the Multiplication of the Loaves and Fishes(Cleveland Museum) is organized as a tripartite composition of the kind found from the 3rd century on in Egyptian painting in the catacombs of Karmuz at Alexandria.[54] Christ,shown standing, is framed by two apostles ; at their feet are

129

**Scenes from the Old Testament
Tapestry. Looped woven wool
5-6 th centuries
3.20 x 3.80 cm**
Bern (Riggisberg), Abegg Stiftung;
inv. 2439
This piece, comparable to
the Jonas tapestry of the
Louvre, was originally
composed of four registers
which mingled figurative
(horsemen, yoke-bearers and
animals), symbolic (crosses
and lamps) and narrative
(ascension of Elijah and
sacrifice of Isaac) images.
The upper register, based on
the model of stelae, is
composed of birds and orans
sheltering under four
arcades.

Nativity
Resist printed linen
Akhmin; 5-6th centuries
47 x 92.5 cm
London, Victoria and Albert
Museum; inv. 1103-1900
The combined technical and
compositional aspects of this
scene establish a connection
between this piece and the
"Voile d'Antionoé" (Louvre).
Semele and the servant girl
could easily be replaced by
the Virgin and an angel. In
the right lower corner it is
possible to make out the
sleeping Child overlooked by
a donkey and an ox.

Page·133 above :
***Orbiculus*. Annunciation and
Visitation**
Silk embroidery on linen
5-6th centuries
D. 19.05 cm
London, Victoria and Albert
Museum; inv. 814-1903
This piece is part of a series
of embroideries of biblical
scenes, conserved in several
different museums, which
might have belonged to a
single item : a liturgical
garment or an altar cloth ?

Detail of the Nativity
See page 129

two large baskets ready to receive the loaves and the fishes

The Woman with the Issue of Blood Touching the Robe of Christ[55] and the Resurrection of Lazurus are combined in a single scene (Victoria and Albert Museum).[56] Christ walks toward Lazurus, swathed in bandages, placed under an aedicule, while the woman with the issue of blood clutches a part of his clothing. This organization is not new, since it is commonly found on the ivories of Early Christian sarcopahagi.

Even if this repertory of Old and New Testament themes on Coptic textiles is not exhaustive, this study reveals that Old Testament scenes are mainly treated on tapestry and, sometimes, printed on linen textiles. Whereas, numerous scenes of the New Testament appear either on silk embroideries on linen cloth or on printed textiles, but rarely on tapestries. The New Testament scenes belong stylistically to the 5th and 6th centuries, and hence to the Byzantine period. The printed textiles are still heavily influenced by Early Christian art and antiquity; embroidered textiles belong to the Byzantine world. Moreover, given the identical nature of the borders composed of rosettes and hearts, it is very possible that several of these embroideries come from the same piece.

A tapestry from the Cleveland Museum of Art,[57] exceptional because of its size and iconography, was virtually treated as an icon by its weaver. The Virgin and Child are seated on a throne set with pearls and colored cabochons. She is flanked on either side by the archangels Michael and Gabriel, whose names, as well as that of Mary, are engraved on an upper lintel supported by two columns with acanthus capitals. They each hold a sword; but in his other hand, Gabriel holds a globe divided into four parts marked by two floral motifs (sun and star) and two crescents. The globe symbolizes the emperors' universal power, in particular, over the missorium* of Theodose I (silver, late 4th century, Academy of History, Madrid).[58] These are also the unusual attributes of archangels or angels, depicted on their own (fragment of an ivory diptych from Constantinople, 6th century, The British Museum; stone pillar from Bawit, 6th century, Louvre).[59] Or in a tripartite composition (silver coathook from Constantinople, late 6th century, Hermitage;[60] limestone reliefs, 6th century, Coptic Museum; Cairo).[61] The icon-like character of this image is established by numerous parallel works, in ivory, carved or painted wood, or in the enthroned Virgin surrounded by religious figures, apostles or angels (painted icon from Constantinople, 6-7th centuries, Saint Catherine, Sinai).[62] This group is surmounted by a Christ enthroned, supported by two

angels, resembling an Ascension. A sumptuous frame of foliage, weighed down by flowers and fruit, contains, at the level of the Virgin, busts of the twelve apostles, each named by a Greek inscription. This organization in two registers is obviously derived from monumental art, the closest models being the apsidal paintings of the "chapels" in the monasteries at Bawit and Saqqara. At Bawit,[63] Christ is often given primary importance and in the conch of an apse, he is represented according to the apocalyptic vision of John or Ezechiel. Christ is enthroned on a chariot of fire, borne by wings of seraphin decorated with eyes and symbols of the Living Four. The Virgin standing or enthroned, is surrounded by evangelists and presented in secondary position in the lower part. On the other hand, at Saqqara, the Virgin is given a prominent position, emphasizing her image as the mother of God and instrument of the Incarnation, as was defined by the Council of Ephesus. Prior to 431, the Virgin appeared in secondary roles; after that date, her iconography is developed to such an extent that she becomes an autonomous figure, especially in the 6th century.

The technical and stylistic quality of this tapestry, with its sculpted faces that contrast with the graphically handled draperies, places it among this period's most accomplished pieces of textile and works of art in general. It is therefore surprising to see the weaver's error in the sizing of the warp which was stretched across width of the tapestry. Since the weaving had begun at the left side of the piece, the weaver was forced to cut the modillon* of the lintel above the archangel Gabriel, who had to be placed in front of the right hand column; moreover, in the upper part, the feet of the angel on the right, overlap onto the border of the frame.

The fragments of a tapestry representing Saint Theodore (Fogg Art Museum, Cambridge, 6t century) are stylistically close to this period. One of the fragments, decorated with foliated scrolls, pearls and cabochons mentions the name of Saint Theodore, while the other contains a bust of the saint (?), holding a long staff with a cross at the end. The portrayal of the subject's face, with its pointed beard, recalls the portrait of Saint Theodore on the painted icon at Saint Catherine in Sinai, where he is depicted with the Virgin and Child and Saint Demetrius.[65] The iconography of these fragments should therefore be resituated in such a context. The remains of a staff on the left side, indicates the presence of another saint, perhaps in a setting similar to that used on the reliefs of the Virgin flanked by four figures, in the Coptic Museum, Cairo.

An inscription in the foliage identifies the figures of Saints Peter and Paul in a square from Berlin.

The Virgin enthroned
Tapestry. Wool
6th century
1.78 x 1.10 m
Cleveland, Museum of Art; inv. 67.144
Conceived as an icon celebrating the glory of the Virgin, this tapestry is composed in form of apsidal decorations. The Virgin occupies a place of primary importance, stressing the preponderant role of the cult of Mary in Christianity and, particularly among the Copts, especially after the Council of Ephesus proclamation concerning the divine maternity. In the upper part, the theme of the Ascension merges with that of apocalyptic theophany, emphasizing the dogma of the Incarnation.

Christ in Glory
Painting
Bawit; 7th century
1 x 1 m
Cairo, Coptic Museum
This apocalyptic vision of
God seated on a throne of
fire, surrouned by seraphim
wings with eyes,is found on
several occasions in Coptic
monasteries. On the lower
part is the Virgin Enthroned
with the Christ Child,
flanked by the apostles. This
composition in two registers
is similar to the Ascension
(page 135) where the
mandorla containing Christ
is lifted by by two angels.

The Saints, dressed in tunics and coats, hold a scroll, representing the Traditio Legis, the Gift of the Law by Christ to the Apostles Peter and Paul, frequently reproduced on sarcophagi (sarcophagus, Louvre, late 4th century).[66]

The fragment of printed linen representing Saints Thomas, Mark and Peter, might be the Communion of the Apostles (Victoria and Albert Museum, 5-6th centuries).[67] The three figures, identified by inscriptions, come forward with their hands veiled as a sign of veneration. A similar scene, depicted on a gilded silver curtain holder from Riha, Syria (Dumbarton Oaks, 6th century),[68] enables us to reconstruct the central figure of Christ between two rows of apostles to whom he is giving communion in the form of bread and wine. Numerous fragments of tapestries depict standing figures of orants or priests. Some of the figures are set in vast architectural compositions resembling stelae decorated with triangular or arched pediments; the conch usually contains a bird (peacock, dove or eagle) while the space between the two columns is filled by the deceased, depicted in prayer or as a saint (looped textile from Akhmin, Abegg Stifftung, 7th century).[69] Beneath a small aedicule with a triangular pediment, a priest appears dressed in a belted tunic, decorated, with bands, epaulettes and squares. (Museum of Fine Arts, Boston, 6th century).[70] He raises a cup with one hand and holds a ladle in the other. Specimens of bronze ladles such as this, dating from the Greek period, have been found in Mediterranean bordering countries. It is possible that this type of instrument was used to draw the holy water for baptism or anointing the faithful. Two other looped woven textiles in the Louvre might be compared. A praying figure near a chandelier, wearing a shawl over a tunic decorated with squares, surmounted by an ankh and the first two letters for God[71] and a piece of textile showing a figure wearing a belted tunic and holding a lighted candelabra in each hand.[72] The theme of the candelabra or lamp, appearing on another piece in the Louvre, next to a large ankh[73] and on a painting in chapel XIX of the monastery at Bawit,[74] indicates its liturgical use in consecrated tombs and funerals of the faithful. These utensils are used to render homage to the defunct and as an image of illumination for the soul's path from earth to heaven. Some terracotta lamps bear symbolic inscriptions, found on all sorts of artifacts, stating, "The light of Christ shines for all."

The figure of the cavalier-saint seems to be a leitmotiv which appears in a variety of forms according to different conceptions. The horse was introduced into Pharaonic Egypt, through Palestine, in the 17th century B.C. The pharaoh and high-ranking dignitaries usually paraded in horse-drawn chariots; horse back riding as such was left to ordinary soldiers. The first example of an Egyptian king charging on horseback occurs in the Ptolemaic period. The only mounted divinity in the Nile Valley is the goddess Astarte, of Oriental origin, adopted by the Egyptians as the "Mistress of the horse and chariot." It is only at a later period that one begins to find other mounted divinities like the horseman, Horus (4-7th centuries).[75]

This theme has two possible iconographical sources. Beginning in the 2nd century B.C., it appeared in the Orient on Thracian votive or funeral stelae, such as the stele, discovered in Theadelphia (Fayum*) bearing the dedication from a temple devoted to the Thracian god, Heron. In the Hellenistic period, equestrian statues of Alexander, and later those of Roman emperors, created an imperial iconography whose most common example is the decoration of Roman triumphal monuments known as the rite of adventus, the solemn entry of the triumphant emperor (Justinian on horseback, Barberini ivory, mid-6th century, Louvre).[76]

The horseman or cavalier is the principal actor in the large mythological battle scenes, such as the combat of giants or amazons (Tunic, late 3rd century A.D., Louvre). In hunting scenes, on sarcophagi, he symbolizes the triumph over death and, by extension, the triumph of Good over Evil; with the advent of Christianity, he represents the victory of new religion over paganism. The emperor was particularly suited to this role of defendor of the new faith and is frequently depicted on horseback, crowned by victory, trampling a symbolic shield (silver Kertch plate, 4th century, Hermitage). The presence of very stylized, and often unrecognizable, shields in Coptic textiles, might also represent matyred saints or anonymous holy persons. The figures appearing on a series of Coptic textiles dating from the 7th century are probably emperors.[77] For the most part, two cavaliers are depicted facing each other, either armed with swords or with a lance piercing a wild beast. The surrounding space is filled with floral elements, wild beasts or dogs attacking animals (The Textile Museum). Silk textiles played a determining role in the elaboration and diffusion of motifs of this kind; the 8th century Moszac silk textile (Musée Historique de Tissus, Lyon) depicts two identical emperors astride magnificent horses plunging their lances into the mouths of two lions. This textile, probably made in the Byzantine period, is evidence of the use of stirrups which had been introduced into the Byzantine cavalry after the victory of the Emperor Heraclius over the Sassanides, in late 6th or early 7th century.

Saint Theodore
Tapestry. Linen and wool
Akhmin ? 4th cnetury
44.1 x 31.8 cm
Cambridge, Massachusetts, Fogg
Art Museum ; inv. 1939.112.1.2.
This figure of Saint
Theodore is so close to the
4-5th century icons that it is
possible to imagine that it
was part of a large tapestry
with several holy figures,
such as the tapestry of the
Virgin Enthroned in the
Cleveland Museum, with
which it shares a similar
style and technique.

One of these textiles, from the Textile Museum in Washington D.C. is distinguished by the arrangement of the two horsemen, wearing stirrups, one on a white horse, the other on a black, each brandishing swords and accompanied by a dog. Two winged putti* hold a crown over their heads, as a distinct mark of the subject's hallowed nature. Another interesting feature of this medallion is the Greek inscription "Alexander the Macedonian" in the upper part. The horses heads, turning towards each other, creates an effect of perspective and likens this example , as well as another held at the Victoria and Albert Museum to a series of carved ivories, probably made in Alexandria and dating from the 6th and 7th centuries (Louvre ; Walters Art Gallery, Baltimore ; Benaki Museum, Athens and Aachen Cathedral). A single horseman (Victoria and Albert Museum) holds a globe in one hand and a sceptre in the other ; he is flanked by two prisoners with their hands tied behind their backs ; underneath the horse, a lion and a dog overpower an animal. On a medallion from the Cooper Union Museum in New York two female dancers replace the prisoners, only a lion appears underneath the horse.

This use of imperial representations gives way to two iconographical types of cavalier-saints. The armed, fighting horseman, evoking the militant triumph of Christianty and the static horseman, surrounded with a halo of his matyrdom or apostate. This motif was particularly valued in Coptic art, since it appears in strictly defined places in numerous monuments. For example, the entrance door of the southern church at Bawit, reconstructed in one of the galleries of the Louvre, is surmounted by a sculpted tympanum decorated with a figure of a cavalier-saint crushing a snake (Saint Sissinnios, 6th century). Chapel XVII, at Bawit, contains paintings of cavalier-saints (6-8th centuries) on its pendentives and on both sides of the niche. The north and western walls of the narthex of the main church of the Convent of Saint Anthony, near the Red Sea, are covered with paintings of ten cavalier-saints (9th century ?).[79]

The "Ascension of Elijah" tapestry from Bern, shows two cavalier-saints with halœs each holding the crown of victory. The motif of cavalier-saints fighting an animal is found on a 9th century medallion in the Louvre. The imagery of the cavalier-saint thrusting his spear into the mouth of a snake is closely related to the representation of the Emperor Constantine, who was the first to be shown trampling a snake in commemoration of his victory over Licinius. The emperor is often replaced by a Christian sign, either a monogram or a cross, piercing the demon, which represents a change from an imagery that is narrative and realistic to one that is symbolic and abstract.

However, neither the presence of the cross in this context nor, that of the crucifixion were ever envisaged by Egyptian Christians. Crucifixion, considered as a particularly harsh punishment, was not represented in Egypt until fairly late (after the 12th century). Whereas the sign of the cross was used to glorify Christ and bear witness to the Christian faith. It was thus repeatedly placed, on both religious and utilitarian monuments, regardless of their function. It appears in various forms, of which the most surprising is the looped cross of Pharaonic origin. The Greek cross with equal, straight or hooked transverse bars, is frequently decorated with geometrical elements in the form of pearls and colored cabochons. Sometimes it appears on its own, or within medallions or squares. A tapestry in the Victoria and Albert Museum shows the cross worn by a winged figure within a sumptuous crown of foliage surrounded by the alpha and the omega.[80] A bird is perched on one of the remaining transverse bars, resembling that found on a sarcophagus of the resurrection (Latran Museum, 4th century). The presence of these birds is not exceptional since several can be seen on tapestries and embroideries. This arrange-

ment also recalls that of the stone stelae where birds are replaced by wild animals or dolphins. Sometimes, the cross is inserted within a foliated scroll similar to the carved friezes in the churches (Bawit, Saqqara, Sohag). It may also be placed under an arcade symbolizing a chapel. In these instances it often takes the form of the latin cross (Louvre) in imitation of certain stelae or stone or wooden lintels.

Crosses containing stylized depictions of what might be the head of Christ are rarer (Victoria and Albert Museum, London).[81] This imagery belongs to a type that can also be found in a painting (a bust of Christ giving benediction, 5th century, Kellia Monastery, Lower Egypt)[82] and a bronze cross (bust of a woman, 7th century, Staatliche Museen, Berlin)[83]. The rarity of this image in Egypt is perhaps explained by the accidental discovery of these objects. In any event, examples are to be found in Rome (mosaic of San Stefano Rotondo); the oratory of the Forty Matyrs in Santa Maria Antiqua in the Forum and at Ravenna, the 6th century mosaic of S. Apollinare in Classe.) This image is also found in Nubia where it was treated in particularly ornate fashion. Christ, giving benediction, is set against the back-

ground of a jewelled cross (Faras painting, 11th century, Warsaw Nationaal Museum). In both Nubia and Egypt, the arms of the cross are linked by small chains with pomegranate shaped pendants and bells hanging from them. The Victoria and Albert Museum possesses two such textiles; one of the crosses has a haft ending with a ball, relating it to bronze processional crosses.

The zenith of Christian iconography on Coptic textiles falls between the 5th and 7th centuries, and corresponds to the period of Byzantine occupation. Beginning in the 8th century, with the profound cultural and religious changes brought about by the Arab contribution, the ornamentation of textiles becomes much more decorative and often stereotyped. The narrative scenes disappear leaving the Christian symbols, crosses and praying figures, which given their function as signs, are lost among the deformed images of foliage, animals, cavaliers, dancers and nereids. "At times there is a real fear of emptiness, meaning that the proportions of the figures stretch to the dimensions of the frame or fill the latter with a crowded abundance of different motifs. Sometimes the proportions of the figure or the ani-

Square with cavaliers. Tapestry. Linen, wool and silk 5-6th centuries
10 x 10 cm
London, Victoria and Albert Museum; inv. 43049
The band of the frame is comparable to the silver handle of a "casserole" in the Hermitage Museum (5-6th centuries). Without being exceptional, the combination of wool, linen and silk, producing a particular brilliance and finesse of execution, is somewhat rare in Coptic tapestries.

Orbiculus* with cavalier killing a serpent
Tapestry. Wool
11th century
18 x 15 cm
Paris, Musée du Louvre, Department of Egyptian Antiquities; inv. E 26518
The cavalier-saint, overpowering a "wicked" animal symbolizes the victory of Good over Evil and Christianity over paganism. The origin of the theme lies in the representaion of imperial victory, which illustrated the triumph of civillization over barbarism.

Orbiculus* with cavalier
Tapestry. Linen and wool
7-8th centuries
34 x 31.5 cm
Washington D.C., The Textile Museum; inv. 11.18
Alexander the Great, represented twice, is being crowned by winged *putti**. The idea of the royal, and then imperial victory, originated from Sassanian hunting scenes and would later be perpetuated by the cult of cavalier-saints.

mals are transformed so that dancers become tumblers or a duck dwarfs the putti that holds it. Sometimes one subject is invaded by another, so that a certian amount of experience is required to distinguish a nereid astride a sea horse from the Parthian cavaliers. Sometimes the stretching of the forms and their divison into geometrical surfaces makes them resemble the figures decorating Peruvian or Mexican textiles. Finally, at times, the parts of the body are very segmented, particularly dancers and cupids. This can be explained by the weaving process itself, but it is taken to an extreme where the legs and arms of a figure are stretched in all possible directions and may be quite far from their owner. All these transformations occur in variations of colors which may be either brilliant or dull, using both the finest and coarsest threads.[85]"

An examination of the history of Egypt between the late 4th to 12th centuries A.D. reveals the extent to which the so-called "Byzantine" period truly constituted the basis of a development that was far from being finished. The study of Coptic textiles confirms this hypothesis when one considers the caesura pro-

voked in the middle of the 7th century. It has been established that a considerable Coptic production continued under Arab govenors. As Pierre du Bourget wrote "... the presence on Coptic tapestries of widely-used motifs, either in the Tulunides or Fatimites textiles, or in the architectonic Muslim decoration of the 10-12th centuries A.D., indicates the extent to which the Muslim influence had penetrated into Coptic life and customs and also throws light on the very special relationship in Egypt uniting the faithful of the two religions.

Nevertheless, it is a fact that the Muslim conquest was an irreparable blow to the fate of Christian art in Egypt, despite the vitality that it showed up until the 12th century. The period which we are obliged to refer to as the "zenith of Coptic art" (5-7th centuries) was only, in fact, a period of maturation similar to the pre-Roman period in the West. "Once in possession of its style, Coptic art could have attained the highest level of artistic achievement with a vision that corresponds astonishingly to Christian symbolism. The Muslim conquest put a halt to this legitimate ambition."[86]

Square with bird
Tapestry, tabby and looped
woven linen
Linen and wool
7th century
77 x 65 cm
Paris, Musée du Louvre,
Department of Egyptian
Antiquities; inv. AF 5510
Squares of this kind,
integrated into backgrounds
of looped woven linen, have
often been identified as
cushion covers. However, it
is more likely that they are
parts of large "blankets"
decorated with several
tapestry squares, imitating
shawls and curtains.

NOTES

1. Pierre du BOURGUET, 1950, p. 35-47.
2. Hayford PIERCE and Royall TYLER, 1934, p. 82 and pl. 44,a.
3. Inv. n° AF5516.
4. Inv. n° AF5639.
5. Albert GAYET, 1905, p. 21.
6. Maurice CHEHAB, 1958, p. 49-50 et pl. XXII-XXV.
7. Susan MACMILLAN ARENSBERG, 1969, p. 90-120.
8. Victor F. LENZEN, 1960, 5, n° 1, pl. 1 (a-b).
9. Inv. n° 90.5.837.
10. Jean CLEDAT, 1915, p. 22-28, pl. II-V.
11. *Un siècle de fouilles françaises en Egypte*, 1981, n° 349, p. 330.
12. François BARATTE, 1985, p. 31-76.
13. Erika SIMON, 1970.
14. Dominique BENAZETH, 1989, p. 219-228.
15. Inv. n° 7004. John BECKWITH, 1963, fig. 68.
16. Ludmila KYBALOVA, 1967, p. 76, n° 25.
17. *Beyond the Pharaohs*, 1989, n° 66, p. 157.
18. François BARATTE, 1978, p. 99-118.
19. Inv. n° E14280.
20. H. LECLERCQ, *D.A.C.L.*, XIV, 1, col.379.
21. *The Royal Hunter*, 1978, p. 37, n° 16 and p. 126, n° 51.
22. *The Royal Hunter*, 1978, p. 130, n° 55; p. 137, n° 61; p. 140, n° 64.
23. *The Royal Hunter*, 1978, p. 80, fig. C (Golden cup, rock crystal and glass, 6th century, Cabinet des Médailles. Bibliothèque nationale).
24. A.F. KENDRICK, 1922, n° 747.
25. Ahmed FAKHRY, 1951, p. 71, fig. 62.
26. Claudia NAUERTH, 1978, p. 105-113.
27. Claudia Nauerth, 1987, p. 135-139.
28. *Age of Spirituality*, 1978, p. 462-463, n° 413.
29. Carlo CECCHELLI, 1944, pl. XVII-XXI.
30. K. WEITZMANN, 1975, p. 70-71.
31. Ahmed FAKHRY, 1951, p. 59, fig. 44.
32. Inv. n° E17071.
33. Inv. n° 51.400.
34. François BARATTE, 1985, fig. 31.
35. Oskar WULFF, 1909, p. 79-80, n° 242.
36. Inv. n° 2439.
37. J.E. QUIBELL, 1912, pl. XII.
38. Oskar WULFF et W.F. VOLBACH, 1923, p. 13, n° 563 and pl. I.
39. *Age of Spirituality*, 1978, p. 433-434, n° 390 and p. 434-435, n° 391.
40. A.F. KENDRICK, 1922, n° 777 and 785.
41. Evangiles apocryphes, p. 75.
42. Inv. n° E 17118.
43. A.F. KENDRICK, 1922, n° 715.
44. A.F. KENDRICK, 1922, n° 786.
45. *Evangiles apocryphes*, p. 81.
46. Carlo CECCHELLI, 1944, pl. XXV.
47. Michael ALPATOFF and Oskar WULFF, 1925, p. 33, Abb.13.
48. Inv. n° 51.400.
49. A.F. KENDRICK, 1922, n° 782.
50. W.F. VOLBACH, 1966, fig. 37.
51. A.F. KENDRICK, 1922, n° 778.
52. A.F. KENDRICK, 1922, n° 781.
53. A.F. KENDRICK, 1922, n° 780.
54. Alexander BADAWY, 1978, fig. 4.14.
55. "And, behold, a woman, who was diseased with an issue of blood twelve years, came behind him, and touched the hem of his garment." (Matthew, 9, 20; Mark, 5, 21; Luke, 8, 42).
56. Inv. n° 722-1897. *Age of Spirituality*, 1978, p. 434-435, n° 391.
57. Dorothy SHEPHERD, 1969, p. 90-120.
58. Hayford PIERCE and Royall TYLER, 1932, p. 46-47, pl. 35, 36, 37.
59. John BECKWITH, 1963, fig. 88 and 89.
60. *Age of Spirituality*, 1978, p. 537-538, n° 482.
61. John BECKWITH, 1963, fig. 111 and 112.
62. *Age of Spirituality*, 1978, p. 533-534, n° 478.
63. Alexander BADAWY, 1978, fig. 4.25, 4.26, 4.27.
64. Alexander BADAWY, 1978, fig. 4.38 and 4.39.
65. *Age of Spirituality*, 1978, p. 533-534, n° 478.
66. Inv. n° MA2980.
67. A.F. KENDRICK, 1922, n° 789.
68. *Age of Spirituality*, 1978, p. 611-612, n° 547.
69. L'art copte, 1964, n° 175.
70. L'art copte, 1964, n° 165.
71. Inv. n° E29307.
72. Inv. n° E10530.
73. Inv. n° E26912.
74. Jean CLEDAT, 1904, fasc.2, pl. LXXV.
75. Klaus PARLASCA, 1982, p. 19-30.
76. André GRABAR, 1936, p. 45-54.
77. Rudolf BERLINER, 1963, p. 39-54.
78. Jean CLEDAT, 1904, fasc.2, pl. XXXIX.
79. Jules LEROY, 1976, p. 347-379.
80. A.F. KENDRICK, 1921, n° 317.
81. A.F. KENDRICK, 1921, n° 320.
82. Marguerite RASSART-DEBERGH, 1981, p. 241-243.
83. Inv. n° 4924.
84. A.F. KENDRICK, 1921, n° 318 and 320.
85. Pierre du BOURGUET, 1960.
86. Pierre du BOURGUET, 1967, p. 193.

APPENDICES

THE DEVELOPMENT OF COLLECTIONS

At the time of Napoleon's campaign in Egypt (1798-1801), the Louvre received its first shipment of objects which were noted on the inventory of the Department of Egyptian Antiquities; the shipments continued until 1857 under Napoleon III. The first textile entries at the British Museum and the Berlin Museum date from the same period.

Excavations, until that time, carried out in anarchic fashion, were officially organized under the aegis of Auguste Mariette (1821-1881) who founded the Boulac Museum in Cairo in 1861. It was, however, Gaston Maspero (1846-1916), his successor as head of the museum, who became interested in Christian sites (Akhmin); discoveries at this site became the core of a collection now at the Coptic Museum which was constructed in 1910 though the collection was moved there only in 1939.

Interest in Coptic collections grew increasingly around this date. In 1882 the Viennese antique dealer, Theodore Graf, created a textile collection which was acquired the same year by the Museum of Vienna.

The Pushkin Museum in Moscow benefited from the acquisitions made by V.G. Bock and V.S. Golenishchev during their voyages in Egypt 1880-1890 while the Hermitage in Leningrad received objects from the excavations carried out by Bock at Akhmin, Aswan and Fayum in 1889.

The Victoria and Albert Museum collections are based on the acquisition in 1886 of approximately 300 textiles from the Akhmin excavations. Numerous other sites, however, such as Antinoopolis, Erment, Hawara (excavations by Flinders Petrie in 1887-88 and 1910-11), Edfu and Abydos yielded objects which entered into the museum's collections in the following years, thereby forming a impressive totality of more than a thousand textiles, including examples from all periods and all techniques.

One of the most important collections of Coptic textiles up until that time came from the excavations carried out by Albert Gayet (1858-1916) at Antinoopolis (Middle Egypt); it forms a large proportion of the Coptic section of the Department of Egyptian Antiquities (Louvre) which now numbers about 4000 pieces. After 1897 Emile Guimet, an industrialist from Lyon directed Albert Gayet to take charge of the excavations which continued until 1910. Sets of objects were then given directly to the Louvre ("Voile d'Antinoé", 1906) but a large part of the objects coming from the excavation belonged to the Musée Guimet, founded in Lyon in 1879 and later transferred to Paris in 1888. It was only in 1947 that the Egyptian collection was given to the Louvre. The excavations, however, having been alternately subsidized by the Musée Guimet, the Chamber of

Commerce of Lyon, the Société du Palais du Costume, the Minister of Public Instruction and Fine Arts and finally by the French Society of Archaeological Excavations, the objects were dispersed in numerous French museums (Musée George Labit in Toulouse, Musée du Perigord at Perigeux, Musée Historique des Tissus in Lyon, les Gobelins, les Arts et Métiers, the Musée de Cluny, the Musée des Arts Décoratifs in Paris and many others!) as well as European museums (University College in London, the Victoria and Albert, the Vatican museums and Berlin museums). After each campaign and before the objects were dispersed, the collections were exhibited at the Musée Guimet. "The collections will be divided amongst several museums. The Louvre, the Decorative Arts, the Gobelins, the Arts et Métiers will each receive their share. Before the dispersion of the collections, the Minister has judged that it will be interesting to present them to the public in their totality in order to establish the stage covered by the research. I give myself the duty to thank it here" (Albert Gayet, *Notice relative aux objets recueillis à Antinœ*, 1901, p.7-8). Dijon, the town where Gayet was born, benefited from the excavations; the Museum of Natural History received a shipment of objects in 1901 and his sister who died in 1924 left her personal collection to the Musée des Beaux Arts.

In 1901 at the Musée Guimet there was a public auction of Egyptian antiquities from the necropolis of Antinoopolis for the benefit of the Société du Palais du Costume which had subsidized the excavations of 1898 and 1900. The sale was divided up in forty one lots, some of which contained more than five hundred pieces; "numerous fragments of embroidery, tapestry, borders, etc. This considerable lot, contained in six crates, will be sold individually and grouped according to the wishes of the interested parties". (Lot 41)

The Musée du Cinquantenaire in Brussels acquired two important collections from the tombs of A. Colluthus and from the "Embroideress". Other pieces went into the collection of Leopold Ikle in Saint Gall.

This dispersion of the objects from Antinoopolis and sites, such as Deir el Dyk, Dronkah, Damietta, Akhmin as well as objects Albert Gayet acquired in sales, into an infinite number of museums made it practically impossible to reassemble the sets. The amplitude of the discoveries remains difficult to evaluate but it is clear that the textiles excavated during this period number several hundreds of thousands.

This phenomenon means that in many cases fragments of the same piece have been divided up into several different collections. The "Tapestry with Fish" is at the Louvre and the Musée Historique des Tissus de Lyon; "Sabine shawl" is at the Louvre, the Musée Historique des Tissus de Lyon and at the Musée des Beaux-Arts, also in Lyon; the orbiculus of gold thread is at the Louvre and at the Musée G. Labit in Toulouse.

Listing all the museums in the world, and they are numerous, which possess Coptic textiles would be tedious and uninteresting. Research on the public collections of Coptic art objects carried out by Pierre du Bourguet provides a quasi-exhaustive list and will be published in The Coptic Encyclopedia (U.S.A.). Objects from excavations, acquired by gift or sale, sometimes form important collections such as those in the Vatican, the Benaki Museum in Athens or the Abegg Stiftung near Berne (Switzerland), are remarkable because of the quality of the pieces. Founded in 1961 by Werner Abegg, the Foundation possesses a most up-to-date conservation laboratory and they have undertaken the restoration of the large printed veil known as "Voile d'Antinoé" (4th century B.C.) in the Louvre; the delicate workmanship necessary to restore the object requires special installations and a superior level of competence.

The large American museums have most frequently formed their collections during the twentieth century. For example, the Textile Museum in Washington D.C. founded by George Hewitt Myers, has acquired since 1925 around four hundred pieces, many of which are of the highest quality.

The Brooklyn Museum possesses several objects from the excavations of the Egypt Exploitation Society in Antinoopolis in 1913-14 but the majority were acquired as gifts or purchases. The Cleveland Museum of Art, the Museum of Fine Arts in Boston as well as the Royal Ontario Museum in Toronto, Canada also followed this pattern.

Countries in the Far East have also become interested in Coptic textiles and they can now be found in Japanese museums. In 1923 S. Akashi, with the authorization of the Kanebo textile company, reassembled a hundred pieces form the collection of Dr F. Fouque (1829-1904); today their numbers have grown to more than five thousand pieces which are conserved in a small private museum built especially for this purpose.

The sale of old collections and contemporary excavations, continues to enrich the museums and to offer both specialists and amateurs a vast field for research and for aesthetic pleasure.

SOME EXAMPLES OF THE DECORATION

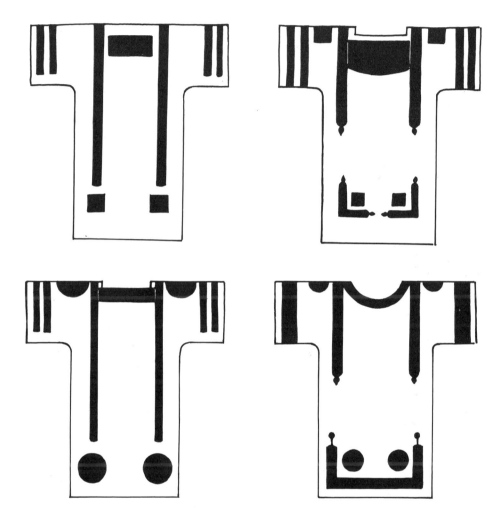

Tunics

Four examples of the decoration of tunics : the clavi,descending from the shoulders in the front and back, sometimes ending with "spearheads." Squares or orbiculi on the shoulders,which are sometimes repeated in the lower part of the clothing where they can be lodged between two angles formed by the clavi at right-angles. On the most decorated examples, the collar is bordered by a large rectangular front that is a pretext for very elaborate and developed scenes.

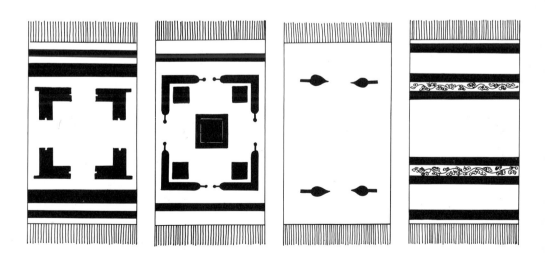

Shawls

As on tunics, the decoration of shawls is extremely varied.They might be decorated with simple clavi bordering the extremities and finished with openwork trimming and fringes.Or, they use the same arrangements found on curtains, altar cloths and blankets : symetric compositions of clavi, orbiculi, squares, elements in the shape of "spearheads" or "leaves" and sometimes scattered flowers.

GLOSSARY

ABYSSINIA
Former name of Ethiopia.

ANCHORITE (Greek anakhorein; to move away)
A religious person who lives in solitude.

APA, ABA (Coptic)
Reverential title given to certain monks or saint.

ASCETIC
A person who dedicates his life to piety and mortifications of the flesh.

AUTOPHAGY
Supporting life with one's own ressources.

BYSSUS (Greek byssos)
Very fine linen.

CENOBITISM (Greek Koinobion = communal life)
The state of being a cenobite; a monk who lives in a community.

CHITON
Greek tunic composed of two rectangular pieces sewn edge to edge vertically; the cloth was fixed on the shoulders and held together with a belt.

CHROMATOGRAPHY
Analysis of colors constituting a material in order to identify it.

CIBORIUM
Canopy above the master of the altar in a church.

CLAVUS (i)
See pp. 54

CROTALUM
Musical instrument composed of a tong, generally in bronze, though very rarely in wood; two small bronze cymbals are inserted between the legs of the tong.

DIOCESE
Territorial district administered by a bishop or archbishop; name for each of the fourteen provinces which composed the Roman Empire in the 4th century.

JALLABEH
A long garment with long sleeves worn by Egyptians today.

KORDOFAN
Region in the Sudan, west of the White Nile.

KUFIC
Ancient form of arabic script.

MISSORIUM
Large piece of silver or gold plate placed as decoration on a table.

MODILLION
Double projecting bracket in the form of an S with unequal curves placed under the molding of a cornice to indicate the end of a rafter.

MOSUL
Town in Iraq on the Tigre.

MUSHARABEYEH
Upper windows in Islamic houses made of elaborate wooden lattices.

NILOMETER
Graded column or staircase to measure the floods on the Nile.

NILOTIC
Relating to the Nile or the adjacent regions.

NOBADES
Nomadic people originating in the desert zones in the west of Egypt; Diocletus introduced them in Nubia; the king of the Nobades converted around 540.

ORBICULUS (i)
see pp. 54

OTHONIA
Vegetal textile material which seems to be very finely woven linen; therefore, this term applies to all fine, light cloth whether it is linen or not.

PENTATEUCH
Name given by Greek translators to the five first books of the Bible.

PORTRAITS OF FAYUM
(1st-4th centuries A.D.).
Small boards or fragments of cloth upon which are painted portraits of the dead; the board was placed on the face of the dead and held in place with small bands; several hundred of these paintings were found in the region of Fayum, hence their name, the Portraits of Fayum.

PUTTO (putti, pl.)
Infants inhabiting certain scenes, particularly, Nilotic scenes.

PYXIS (from Greek puxis, box)
Small wooden box which had many uses; the term extends to jewelry boxes in precious wood, ivory, gold, often ornamented with engravings and reliefs.

SAMITE
Term used for rich medieval silk fabric interwoven with gold and silver.

SASSANID
Dynasty which reigned from 224 to 651 A.D. over an empire including Iran, Iraq, part of Armenia, Georgia, Afghanistan and southern Central Asia. At times they extented their conquests to the eastern coast of the Mediterranean and established their suzerainty over Egypt.

SENNAR
Town in the Sudan on the Blue Nile.

SERAPEUM
Name of temples consecrated to the Egyptian
god Serapis; the most well-known are those in
Alexandria and Memphis.

SHOOT (weft)
Back and forth of a weft thread across the warp
threads.

SITULE
A bucket for libations with a handle for
suspension; used in the cult of the gods and for
the dead.

SPECTROPHOTOMETRY
Analysis of specters constituting a material for
identificating purposes.

SPRANG
see p. 32

SWASTIKA
A cross in the form of a Greek cross with the
ends of the arms extended at right angles in the
same direction

TABULA (ae)
see p 54

TAQUETE
A complex textile of which the background and
the decoration are produced by threads regularly
linked in taffeta which creates a flat look.

THIASE (bacchic)
A religious brotherhood placed under the
patronage of a god, particularly Dionysus, which
forms a noisy group with singing, dancing and
shouting.

URAEUS (pl. uraei)
A cobra representing the goddess personifying
the burning eye of Re (the sun) and symbolizing
the fiery nature of the crown of Upper and
Lower Egypt.

INDEX

BIBLIOGRAPHY

A.S.A.E. : Annales du Service des antiquités de l'Egypte.

B.I.F.A.O. : Bulletin de l'Institut français d'archéologie orientale.

B.S.A.C. : Bulletin de la Société d'archéologie copte.

B.S.F.E. : Bulletin de la Société française d'égyptologie.

C.I.E.T.A. : Centre international d'études des textiles anciens.

D.A.C.L. : Dictionnaire d'archéologie chrétienne et de liturgie.

I.F.A.O. : Institut français d'archéologie orientale.

J.E.A. : Journal of Egyptian Archaeology.

M.I.F.A.O. : Mémoires de l'Institut français d'archéologie orientale.

Age of Spirituality. Exhibition at the Metropolitan Museum of Art, November 1977-February 1978.

AKASHI Kunisuke, *Coptic Textiles from Burying-Grounds in Egypt in the Collection of Kanegafuchi Spinning Company*, Kyoto-Shoin 1955.

AMELINEAU E., *Monuments pour servir à l'histoire de l'Egypte chrétienne*, Report published by the members of the French archaeological expedition to Cairo, Paris, IV, 1888.

BACHATLY Charles, *Le monastère de Phaebammon dans la Thébaïde*, Le Caire, Publications de la Société d'archéologie copte, III, 1961.

BADAWY Alexander, *Coptic Art and Archeology*, The Massachusetts Institute of Technology, Cambridge, 1978.

BAGINSKI Alisa and TIDHAR Amalia, *Textiles from Egypt 4th-13th Centuries C.E.*, L.A. Mayer Memorial Institute for Islamic Art, Tel Aviv, 1980.

BAILLET Jules, *Les tapisseries d'Antinoé au musée d'Orléans*, Orléans, 1907.

BARATTE François,

– *Catalogue des mosaïques romaines et paléochrétiennes du musée du Louvre*, Paris, R.M.N., 1978.

– "Héros et chasseurs : la tenture d'Artémis de la Fondation Abegg à Riggisberg" in *Monuments et mémoires. Fondation Eugène Piot*, P.U.F., 1985, 67, p.31-76.

BECKWITH John,

– "Tissus coptes" in *Les cahiers CIBA*, VII, n°83, août 1959 p.2-27.

– *Coptic Sculpture 300-1300*, London, Alec Tiranti, 1963.

BELLINGER Louisa, "Textile Analysis : Early Techniques in Egypt and the Near East" in *Workshop Notes – The Textile Museum*, June 1950, paper n°2.

BENAZETH Dominique, "Un rare exemple de tissu copte à fil d'or" in *Tissage, corderie, vannerie-IXᵉ Rencontres Internationales d'Archéologie et d'Histoire*, Antibes, octobre 1988, Editions A.P.D.C.A., Juan-les-Pins, 1989, p.219-228.

BERGMAN Ingrid, *Late Nubian Textiles*, The Scandinavian joint expedition to Sudanese Nubia, 8, Lund, 1975.

BERLINER Rudolf, "Horsemen in Tapestry Roundels Found in Egypt" in *Textile Museum Journal*, 1 (2), December 1963, p.39-54.

Beyond the Pharaohs. Exhibition at the Museum of Art, Rhode Island School of Design, 1989.

BOUCHET Dominique, *L'expression "Dalmatique copte" est-elle acceptable ?*, Dissertation for the Ecole du Louvre under the direction of Pierre du Bourguet, Paris, 1981 (unpublished).

BOURGUET (du) Pierre,

– "Survivances pharaoniques dans quelques tissus coptes du musée du Louvre" in *B.S.F.E.*, n°4, octobre 1950, p.35-47.

– "La fabrication des tissus coptes aurait-elle largement survécu à la conquête arabe ?" in Bulletin de la Société archéologique d'Alexandrie, 1953, 40, p.1-31.

– "Un groupe de tissus coptes d'époque musulmane" in *Cahiers de Byrsa (Carthage)*, III, 1953, p.167-174.

– "Carbone 14 et tissus coptes" in *Bulletin du Laboratoire du musée du Louvre*, n° 2, octobre 1957, p.1-31.

– "Datation des tissus coptes et Carbone 14" *Ibid.*, n°3, juin 1958, p.52-63.

– "Actualité des tapisseries coptes" in *Cahiers de la tapisserie*, Paris, Galerie d'Aubusson, juin 1960.

– *Musée National du Louvre Catalogue des étoffes coptes*, I, Paris, R.M.N., 1964.

– *L'art copte*, Paris, Albin Michel, 1967.

BOVOT Jean-Luc, "Le vêtement égyptien" in *Tissu et vêtement 5000 ans de savoir-faire*, exhibition at the Musée archéologique départemental du Val-d'Oise, Guiry-en-Vexin, 1986, p.74-80.

Catalogue des livres d'heures enluminés... Recueil d'étoffes coptes du IIIᵉ s. et souvenirs des fouilles d'Antinoé..., Paris, Hôtel Drouot, Jeudi 23 février 1928, n°26.

CECCHELLI Carlo, *La Cattedra di Massimiano*, R. Istituto di archeologia e storia dell'arte, Roma, 1944.

CHEBAB Maurice, *Mosaïques du Liban*, Bulletin du musée de Beyrouth, XIV, Paris, Librairie d'Amérique et d'Orient, Adrien Maisonneuve, 1958.

Cincinnati Modern Art Society Marsden Hartley-Stuart Davis October 24 to November 24, 1941, Exhibition catalog with text by Hartley.

CLEDAT Jean,

– *Le monastère et la nécropole de Baouît*, M.I.F.A.O., Le Caire, XII, fasc. 2, 1904 ; XXXXIX, 1916.

– "Fouilles à Cheikh Zouède (janvier-février 1913)" in *A.S.A.E.*, 1915, p.15-48.

– "Baouît" in *D.A.C.L.*, II, 1, col. 203-251.

Collection du docteur Fouquet du Caire, 2, Catalogue des Antiquités Egyptiennes séries coptes et arabes, auction 19-20 June, Paris, 1922.

COLLINGWOOD P., *The Techniques of Sprang. Plaiting on Stretched Threads*, London, Faber, 1974.

Coptic art, Exhibition of Coptic Art by the Olsen Foundation, Nov. Déc. 1955 : "Coptic Art A Stimulus to the Creative Impulse of the modern Artist," by Nanette B. Rodney.

CROWFOOT G.M. and GARIES DAVIES (de) N., "The tunic of Tutankhamum" in *J.E.A.*, 1941, 26, p.113-138.

DIEHL Charles, "L'Egypte chrétienne et byzantine" in Gabriel Hanotaux, *Histoire de la Nation égyptienne*, Paris, 3, 1933.

DILLMONT (de) Thérèse, *Motifs de broderie copte, l'art chrétien en Egypte*, Th. de Dillmont, Editeur, Dornach (Alsace), 3 fascicules non datés.

DIMAND Maurice S., *Die Ornamentik der Agyptischen Wollwirkereien*, Leipzig, 1924.

DONADONI-ROVERI A.M., "Fouilles dans le musée de Turin", in *Actes du Iᵉʳ congrès international d'égyptologie*, Le Caire, 1976, p.181-192.

DUNAND Françoise et LICHTENBERG Roger, "Une tunique brodée de la nécropole de Douch" in *B.I.F.A.O.*, 1985, 85, p.133-148, pl.XXII-XXVII.

EFFENBERGER Arne, *Koptische Kunst*, Leipzig, Kœhler und Amelang, 1975.

FAKHRY Ahmed, *The Necropolis of El-Bagawat*, Service of Egyptian Antiquities, Cairo, Le Caire, 1951.

FORBES R.J., *Studies in Ancient Technology*, Leiden, E.J. Brill, IV, 1956.

GAYET Albert,

– *Catalogue des objets recueillis à Antinoé*, Paris, Musée Guimet, 1898.

– *Notice relative aux objets recueillis à Antinoé*, Paris, Ernest Leroux éditeur, 1900.

– *Catalogue sommaire* – Société Française des Fouilles Archéologiques, First exhibition June-July 1905, Petit Palais des Champs-Elysées.

GERSPACH Edouard,

– "Les tapisseries coptes du Musée des Gobelins" in *Gazette des Beaux-Arts*, 1887, p.125-131.

– *Les tapisseries coptes*, Paris, Maison Quantin, 1890.

GRABAR André, *L'Empereur dans l'art byzantin*, Paris, Les Belles Lettres, 1936.

GUERRINI Lucia, *Le stoffe copte del museo archeologico di Firenze (Antica collezione)*, Roma 1957.

GUIMET Emile, "Les récentes découvertes archéologiques faites en Egypte" in *Conférences faites au musée Guimet*, Paris, Ernest Leroux Editeur, 1905, p.35-91.

Les portraits d'Antinoé au musée Guimet, Paris, Annales du musée Guimet, 1913.

KENDRICK A.F., *Catalogue of Textiles from Burying-Grounds in Egypt*, Victoria and Albert Museum, London, I, 1920 ; III, 1922.

Koptische Gewerbe. Industrie und Gewerbemuseum des Kaufmännischen Directoriums St Gallen, 1981.

KÜHNEL Ernst, "La tradition copte dans les tissus musulmans" in *B.S.A.C.*, 1938, IV, p. 79-89.

KYBALOVA Ludmila, *Les tissus coptes*, Paris, Edition Cercle d'Art, 1967.

LAFONTAINE-DOSOGNE Jacqueline, *Textiles coptes*, Musées Royaux d'Art et d'Histoire, Bruxelles, 1988.

La rime et la raison, The Ménil Collections (Houston-New York), R.M.N., Galeries Nationales du Grand Palais, Paris 17 avril-30 juillet 1984.

L'Art copte, Exhibition Petit-Palais, Paris, 1964.

LECLERCQ H.,

– "Perle" in *D.A.C.L.*, XIV, 1, col.379-383.

– "Tissu" in *D.A.C.L.*, XV, 2, col.2407-2416.

Le costume en Egypte du IIIè au XIIIè siècle d'après les fouilles de M.A. Gayet, Palais du Costume, Exposition Universelle de 1900, Paris 1900.

LEE CAROLL Diane, *Looms and Textiles of the Copts-First Millenium Egyptian Textiles in the Carl Austin Rietz Collection of the California Academy of Sciences*, 1988.

LENZEN Victor F., "The Triumph of Dionysus on Textiles of Late Antique Egypt" in *University of California Publications in Classical Archaeology*, 1960, 5, n°1, p.1-23.

LEROY Jules, "Le programme décoratif de l'église de Saint-Antoine du désert de la Mer Rouge" in *B.I.F.A.O.*, 76, 1976, p.347-379.

LEVI Doro, *Antioch Mosaic Pavements*, Princeton, I, 1947.

LEWIS Suzanne, *Early Coptic Textiles*, Stanford Art Gallery, Stanford University, May 4-25, 1969.

MACMILLAN ARENSBERG Susan, "Dionysus : A Late Antique Tapestry", in *Boston Museum Bulletin*, 75, 1977, p. 4-25.

MARTINIANI-REBER Marielle, *Lyon, musée Historique des Tissus Soieries sassanides, coptes et byzantines Vᵉ-XIᵉ siècles*, Paris, R.M.N., 1986.

MASPERO Jean, *Histoire des patriarches d'Alexandrie*, Paris, Bibliothèque de l'Ecole des Hautes Etudes, 1923.

MORFIN Nicole, *Le costume religieux chez les Coptes*, Dissertation for the Ecole du Louvre under the direction of Pierre du Bourguet, Paris, 1983 (unpublished).

NAUERTH Claudia,

– "Die Josefsgeschichte auf koptischen Stoffen" in *Enchoria*, Wiesbaden, VIII, 1978, p.105-113.

– "Bemerkungen zum koptischen Josef" in *Rivista degli studi orientali*, Roma, LVIII, fasc. I-IV (1984), 1987, p.135-139.

– *Koptisch Stoffe*, Liebieghaus Monographie, Band 9, Frankfurt am Main 1986.

PARLASCA Klaus, "Pseudokoptische "Reiterleilige" in *Studien zur Spätantiken und Frühchristlichen Kunst und Kultur des Orients*, Wiesbaden, 1982, p.19-30.

PAUTY Edmond, *Bois sculptés d'église coptes*, Le Caire, I.F.A.O. 1930.

PERDRIZET Paul, "La tunique liturgique historiée de Saqqara" dans *Monuments et mémoires*, Fondation Eugène Piot, P.U.F., 1934, XXXIV, p.97-128.

PETRIE W.M. Flinders, Hawara, *Biahmu and Arisnoë*, London, 1889.

PFISTER Dominique, *Le costume civil copte, ses composantes et son évolution*, Dissertation for the Ecole du Louvre under the direction of Pierre du Bourguet, Paris (unpublished).

PFISTER Rodolphe,

– "Etudes textiles" in *Revue des Arts asiatiques*, 1934, p.77-92.

– *Textiles de Palmyre*, Paris, les éditions d'art et d'histoire, I, 1934 ; II, 1937 ; III, 1940.

– "Teinture et alchimie dans l'orient hellénistique" in *Seminarium Kondakovianum*, VII, Institut Kondakov, Praha, 1935.

PFISTER Rodolphe and BELLINGER Louisa, *The Excavations at Dura-Europos, Part II, The Textiles*, New Haven Yale University Press 1945.

PICARD-SCHMITTER Marie-Thérèse, "Recherches sur les métiers à tisser antiques à propos de la frise du forum de Nerva à Rome" in *Latomus*, 1965, 24, 2, p.296-321.

PIERCE Hayford et TYLER Royall, *L'art byzantin*, Paris, I, 1932 ; II, 1934.

QUIBELL J.E., Excavations at Saqqara (1907-1908), Le Caire, I.F.A.O., 1909 ; (1908-1909, 1909-1910), Le Caire, I.F.A.O., 1912.

RASSART-DEBERGH Marguerite, "La peinture copte avant le XIIᵉ sicèle. Une approche" in *Acta Ad archaeologiam et artium historiam pertinentia*, IX, Roma, 1981, p.221-285.

RAVIDOUT Maurice, "La toilette d'une élégante d'antinoé" dans *Fémina*, p.621-622.

RENNER Dorothée,

– *Die koptischen Stoffe im Martin von Wagner Museum der Universität Würzburg*, Wiesbaden, 1974.

– *Die koptischen Textilien in den Vatikanischen Museen*, Franz Steiner Verlag, Wiesbaden, 1982.

– *Die Spätantiken und koptischen Textilien im Hessischen Landsmuseum in Darmstadt*, Otto Harrassowitz, Wiesbaden 1985.

RIEFSTAHL E., *Patterned Textiles of the Pharaonic Period*, Brooklyn, 1944.

RUTSCHOWSCAYA Marie-Hélène,

– *Tissage et tissus coptes*. Musée du Louvre, Petits guides des grands musées, 58, Paris, 1979.

– "Le tissu dans l'ameublement" in *Tissu et vêtement*

5000 ans de savoir-faire, exhibition au Musée archéologique départemental du Val-d'Oise, Guiry-en-Vexin, 1986, p.142-143.

– *Musée du Louvre – Bois de l'Egypte copte*, Paris, R.M.N., 1986.

– "Le matériel du tisserand égyptien d'après les collections du musée du Louvre" dans Rivista degli Studi Orientali, Roma, 1987, LVIII, fasc. I-IV (1984), p.153-172.

– "Le tissage dans l'Egypte chrétienne – Etat de la question" dans Artistes, artisans et production artistique au Moyen-Age, colloque international, Renne II (2-6 mai 1983), commande et travail, Paris, Picard, 1987, p.477-488.

– "Réorganisation des collections textiles coptes du musée du Louvre – Etat et perspective" dans *Musées et collections publiques de France*, n°178, 1988-1, p.39-40.

SCHNEIDER Pierre, *Matisse*, New York, Rizzoli, 1984.

SEAGROATT Margaret, *Coptic weaves*. City of Liverpool Museums, 1965.

SHEPHERD Dorothy, "An Icon of the Virgin" in *The Bulletin of the Cleveland Museum*, LVI, 3, March 1969, p.90-120.

SHURINOVA R., *Coptic Textiles – Collection Textiles State Pushkin Museum of Fine Arts*, Moscow, 1967.

SIMON Erika, *Meleager und Atalante*, Abegg-Stiftung, Bern 1970.

Sublime indigo, Marseille, Centre de la Vieille Charité, 22 March-31 May 1987.

Textilien aus Agypten im Museum Rietberg Zürich, Zürich 1976.

The Royal Hunter – Art of the Sassanian Empire, exhibition at Asia House Gallery, New York City, 1978.

THOMPSON Deborah, *Coptic Textiles in the Brooklyn Museum*, New York, 1971.

TRILLING James, *The Roman Heritage – Textiles from Egypt and the Eastern Mediterranean 300 to 600 A.D.*, The Textile Museum, Washington D.C., 1982.

Un siècle de fouilles françaises en Egypte 1880-1980, Ecole du Caire (IFAO) Musée du Louvre. Exhibition Musée d'Art et d'Essai-Palais de Tokyo, 1981.

VIAL Gabriel, "Deux exemplaires d'utilisation de soie non-mûrier (Tussah) dans les tissus anciens" in *Bulletin de liaison du C.I.E.T.A.*, 1985, n°61-62, p.50-53.

VOLBACH W.F., *Il tissuto nell'arte antica*, Fratelli Fabbri Editori, Milano, 1966.

WEITZMANN K., "The Selection of texts for Cyclic Illustration in Byzantine Manuscripts" in *Byzantine Books and Bookmen*, Washington, 1975, 1975, p.69-109.

WINLOCK H.E. et CRUM W.E., *The Monastery of Epiphanius at Thebes*, New York, The Metropolitan Museum of Art, 1926.

WIPSZYCKA Ewa, *L'industrie textile dans l'Egypte romaine*, Warszawa, 1965.

WULFF Oskar, *Altchristliche und Mittelaterliche Byzantinische und Italienische Bildwerke*, I, Berlin, 1909.

WULFF Oskar et ALPATOFF Michael, *Denkmäler der Ikonenmalerei*, Dresden, 1925.

WULFF Oskar et VOLBACH W.F., *Die Altchristlichen und Mittelalterlichen Byzantinischen und Italienischen Bildwerke*, Berlin und Leipzig, 1923.

WULFF Oskar et VOLBACH W.F., *Spätantike und koptische Stoffe aus ägyptischen Grabfunder in den Staatlichen Museen*, Berlin, 1926.

PHOTOGRAPHIC CREDITS

Abbreviations : a = above ; b = below ; l = left ; r = right.

Diagrams by Claire Lefèbvre.
Map (p.6) by Nathalie Couthon.
Reconstruction of the "Voile d'Antinoé" (p.28) by Regula Schorta.

B.N. : 26, 63.
Caetano, Philippe : 12, 14-15, 17, 34, 35, 41, 55, 56, 72, 81, 103, 108 al, 109, 112, a, 115, 123 l, cover.

Hatala, Béatrice : 3, 4, 5, 20, 22, 24, 27, 33, 42, 48, 49, 50, 51, 52, 53, 59, 60-61, 66, 67, 70, 73, 75, 79, 80, 92, 94, 95, 98, 102, 107, 108 bl, 117 b, 119, 122, 123 r, 126-127, 129 b, 133 b, 142, 145, cover vignettes.

MUSEUMS

Athens, Benaki Museum : 93.
Berlin, Früchristlich-byzantinische Sammlung : 45, 140.
Bern, Abegg-Stiffung : 20, 28, 29, 69 r and b.l, 83, 84-85, 86, 100, 111 rm, 130-131. Elsa Bloch-Diener, Antike Kunst : 99.
Boston , Museum of Fine Arts : 19, 87 l.
Brussels, Musées Royaux d'Art et d'Histoire : 47 (Christel Valkenberg).
Cairo, Coptic Museum : 96, 111 l, 136.
Cambridge (Massachusetts), Fogg Art Museum : 138
(courtesy of The Arthur M. Sackler fund, Harvard University ; gift Mrs John D. Rockefeller, Jr.)
Cleveland, Museum of Fine Art : 71, 87 r, 135 (purchase, Leonard C. Hanna Jr. bequest).
Frankfurt, Museum für Kunsthandwerk : 116 b.
Haifa : 9.
London : British Museum : 69 a.l, 101. Victoria and Albert Museum : 7, 37, 116 a, 132, 133 a, 141.
Lyon : Musée Historique des Tissus : 16, 57, 68, 129 a.
New York : The Brooklyn Museum : 104, 105, 117 a.
The Metropolitan Museum of Art : 88-89 (gift of Edward S. Harkness, 1931) ; 90 (gift of George F. Baker, 1890).
Osaka, Kanegafuchi Spinning Company : 96 (the Kunebo collection).
Paris, Musée du Louvre : 110, 112 b.l, 136 (Jean-Luc Bovot).
Réunion des Musées nationaux : 114.
Prague, Museum of Decorative Arts : 91 (Miloslav Sebek).
Saint Louis, The Art Museum : 106.
Torino, Museo Egizio di Torino : 40.
Trier, Stadtmuseum : 125.
Trieste, Museo Civico : 120.
Washington D.C., Dumbarton Oaks Collection : 64, 118, 121.
The Textile Museum : 38, 39, 65, 76, 113, 143.

Project editor Monique Lévi-Strauss

Design by Pascale Ogée
Composition by Union Lino, Paris
Photœngraving by Cromolito, Milan
Printed and bound by Mondadori, Verona